WHAT PEOPLE ARE SAYING...

"Mark's sage advice to small business owners navigating tax planning is worth its weight in gold."

—CLATE MASK, CEO, INFUSIONSOFT

"Mark's book offers outstanding tax strategies that will help you bring your American Dream to life! I loved it!"

—KRISTA BLOOM, PH.D., AUTHOR OF *THE ULTIMATE COMPATIBILITY QUIZ*

"Mark is no ordinary CPA; he actually makes the topic of taxes interesting and fun to learn about"

—ELLIE KAYE, AUTHOR OF *LIVING RICH FOR LESS*

"Mark's enthusiasm and passion for a topic usually associated with pain and grief is only matched by his expertise and ability to break down complex principles into simple actionable steps. This is a must-read for any business owner or entrepreneur."

—BRYAN ELLIOTT, FOUNDER, LINKED ORANGE COUNTY

"Mark is a brilliant writer whose uncanny ability to weave educational principles into engaging stories has made him one of my favorite authors. This book is a must-read for anyone interested in saving or making money. I have recommended it to all of our staff and customers alike."

—BOB SNYDER, RENATUS, LLC

"I've been an investor for 15 years and was always taught my NETWORK is equal to my NETWORTH. If you are serious about creating a great NETWORTH, then you must have Mark and his team as part of your NETWORK for tax and legal support. My business and family thank you, Mark, and wish we would have met you 15 years ago."

—CHRIS D. HAKE, REHAS-R-US

"Mark is a very gifted and inspiring man. He has such an ability to connect with everyone he meets and teaches vast knowledge and skills to the common person. Since taking his tax and legal classes I have saved over $30 thousand with different tax incentives and have made even more knowing how to embrace the different tax and legal strategies. What I like best about Mark is that he operates with the highest of integrity, and I know that I am in great hands when he is assisting me."

—CHASE DIXON, DIRECTOR OF MARKETING, THE OG MANDINO GROUP INC.

"Mark has me jumping out of my seat and ready to rock and roll my taxes and the law. Now that's takes skill with the law and a special rapport with people ..."

—VINCE GREAVES, INNOVATIVE PROPERTY SOLUTIONS, INC.

"We attended two classes on taxes taught by Mark and the amount of information I got from them was and still is priceless. My husband and I got more organized in our businesses expenses, like Mark said, and the end result was impressive. After seeing Mark in action, we decided to become his clients and Mark became our tax attorney. Let me tell you, in our first tax return we recovered Mark's fee and MORE, just because we were aware of what to do."
—FRANK & AIDA DODARO, F&A ENTERPRISES, INC.

"Mark is an extremely intelligent individual who makes complex issues simple. I now use Mr. Kohler as my legal and tax planning professional."
—TONY LEENKNECHT, LEENKNECT FINANCIAL SERVICES, INC.

"I had the pleasure of attending one of Mark's workshops and couldn't recommend him more highly. He offers brilliant advice, and he has the unique ability to teach in a manner that everyone can understand. The knowledge he shares with everyone is amazing and he has a staff behind him that is second to none."
—KAREN HALABY, KARADA MARKETING, INC.

"My husband and I attended Mark Kohler's seminar and were just awestruck. We loved that he could provide both an attorney and CPA perspective to our real estate holdings. His office is now handling our taxes and we will begin working on asset protection shortly. We are very impressed with Mark as a speaker because he is so knowledgeable, entertaining, and charismatic. We walked away with value from his seminar."
—MICHELLE BRODERSON, MICHELLE BRODERSON, INC.

"Mark is unique in that he has found a way to make a boring subject fun and entertaining, using stories and analogies and dancing! Yes it's true a person can be competent/professional and laugh!! It was so hard inviting people to an all-day Saturday 'tax and legal' workshop; they looked at me like huh? But those that came had an amazing time."
—CHRISTINA HAFTMAN, SOCIAL MEDIA STRATEGIES 4 YOU

"I have been in several of Mark's classes,, and I have used his company for accounting. In the last three years he has saved us thousands of dollars. His classes are so entertaining and he is very knowledgeable on the subject of tax law for real estate. He is able to make his classes enjoyable despite the subject. I can't wait until he comes to Chicago again."
—GENE MACKIN, 4 CAPITAL RESULTS, INC.

WHAT YOUR CPA ISN'T TELLING YOU

LIFE-CHANGING
TAX STRATEGIES

MARK J. KOHLER
CPA, ATTORNEY AT LAW

Entrepreneur.
Press

Jere L. Calmes, Publisher
Cover Design: Andrew Welyczko
Production and Composition: Eliot House Productions

This publication is designed to provide accurate and authoritative information
in regard to the subject matter covered. It is sold with the understanding that
the publisher is not engaged in rendering legal, accounting or other professional
services. If legal advice or other expert assistance is required, the services of a
competent professional person should be sought.

Library of Congress Cataloging-in-Publication Data
Kohler, Mark J.
    What your CPA isn't telling you: life-changing strategies by Mark J. Kohler.
        p.   cm.
    ISBN-10: 1-59918-416-8 (alk. paper)
    ISBN-13: 978-1-59918-416-6 (alk. paper)
        1. Finance, Personal. 2. Investments. 3. Income tax. I. Title.
    HG179.K6235 2011
    332.024—dc22   2010046013

Printed in Canada

15 14 13 12   10 9 8 7 6 5 4 3 2 1

This book is dedicated to taxpayers trying to live the American Dream and who doesn't know where to turn for meaningful tax planning.

CONTENTS

CONCEPT 4

TECHNIQUES IN **BUSINESS PLANNING** 57

CONCEPT 5

RENTAL **REAL ESTATE** 75

CONCEPT 6

LEAVING A **LEGACY** 93

CONCEPT 7

YOUR **HEALTH CARE** 109

"Insanity: doing the same thing over and over again and expecting different results."

—ALBERT EINSTEIN

ACKNOWLEDGMENTS

I don't think people realize how hard it is to write a book and how many people work behind the scenes to make it a success. I say this, because I had no idea what an enormous undertaking it was to write my first book and then had selective memory when I was enjoying the success of *Lawyers Are Liars*. I forgot how much work it really was.

This book was even harder for me to write because it forced me well beyond my comfort level with writing, and I got exposed to the art of fictional writing. I couldn't have accomplished this huge undertaking without the unfailing support of my wife and children. They were consistently supportive when I took hours away from them to sit in coffee shops in the evening and escape to any quiet place I could to write. My love and desire to help them succeed in their own endeavors has only grown during this process.

Again, my partners and team members at the law firm and accounting firm truly help me be the best I can be as a professional. More specifically, Mat Sorensen and LaDell Eyre continue to be pillars of strength to me and have become eternal friends.

Special thanks to my publicist Melanie Thomas and her amazing skills at making a CPA interesting to talk with and look at. Also to Jason and Shelley Andrus, and Julie Fletcher for their editorial comments and review.

With all of that said, this book's quality and success is directly related to the enormous support, encouragement, and cooperation from my publisher Entrepreneur Press. Their willingness to take a leap of faith on such a unique book about taxes was truly visionary.

AN ELUSIVE DREAM

I am convinced that millions of Americans are starving for tax advice, but the shocking reality is that many don't know where to turn for answers.

Taxes are the number-one cost in our lives. We know this. But for some reason we believe that the topic is either too boring or complex to be worth investing any time into. Hell, I felt the same way even after I was a CPA.

However, after teaching and advising thousands of clients, I have discovered that there are several, if not many, things CPAs don't know or just don't tell their clients for one reason or another—information that would change their clients' tax returns and their lives!

Maybe it's because they are poor communicators. Maybe we don't give them a chance. Maybe it's because we believe deep down that our tax return "is what it is," and there is nothing we can really do to change the bottom line. Whatever the reasons are, I know there are tax strategies that can change your life.

Now with that said, I face the daunting task of writing a book that you might actually want to read and share with your loved ones.

What are these tax strategies and guiding principles that don't change every year with new legislation? What is it that my CPA should be telling me in a planning meeting each year, or even more often than that?

I chose the medium of a story to convey this essential information.

It's actually a fairly short story to tell. Call it a fable, an allegory, or parable. The bottom line is that whatever you call it, it's the saga of how a group of individuals found answers to one of life's biggest challenges in an unlikely place.

The story starts with a fictional family that may seem very similar to yours. Now, please know I'm not talking about the resemblance to any particular family structure, but the similarities in the challenges that we all face living here in the great United States of America.

Of course, I realize that all of us come from many different walks of life. And clearly, the modern American family isn't so traditional anymore, is it?

What this means is whether we like to admit it or not, we have single parents, inter-racial marriages, same-sex couples, no kids, good kids, and even bad kids, or should I say kids not living up to their potential. Apparently that's the politically correct way to say it. With all of that said, you may still find this story conventional and even familiar.

There is a common challenge all the characters in this story face: the challenge of making a living. How to have a little extra money once in a while to spend on the things we enjoy, build a retirement fund for some day in the future, and along the way pay for the largest expense of our lives: taxes.

As I've met with thousands of clients over the years, it has been interesting to discover that many of them, including my family and friends, have consistently summed up this quest in the simple phrase "Trying to live the Dream."

The meaning of the American Dream, of course, can be debated for hours on end and has been described countless ways. However, it doesn't have to mean being retired and sipping margaritas on some beautiful beach or mountaintop. Maybe it's just having a little more balance in life and not having to consistently stress about finances.

No matter how you define this quest, no matter what political party you align yourself with, we can agree: The Dream is an elusive one to millions of Americans today.

When I first started practicing as a CPA and attorney, I thought I had found my calling. I felt I was helping people, and I truly enjoyed the work. However, I had no idea that the concept of tax planning could actually change lives—really change lives in a meaningful way.

I realized this when more and more clients ended up on my doorstep looking for basic "life" planning as they tried to find the American Dream.

They didn't have anywhere else to turn. They would tell me that if they wanted some "coaching" or "education" on how to get ahead in the game, they would turn to a good book.

They weren't going to call their financial planner—although he or she would be a great resource on how to build their retirement, invest cash, or maybe get the right mortgage. But the traditional financial planner didn't have the tools to help them climb the corporate ladder any faster or start the right small business, and they certainly weren't going to bring up the topic of real estate.

Meet with their lawyer? Most lawyers aren't trained or have the expertise to run a real business. They just solve problems, or hopefully prevent them from happening. The insurance agent? The banker? Give me a break! They all have specific agendas, and thinking outside of the box and giving practical strategies about building wealth aren't their strong points.

I suppose that left just the CPA, the person that they should certainly have as part of their team, but who most struggle to have a meaningful conversation with at any point during the year. Come on . . . we have a better chance of communicating with a taxi driver in New York City than with our accountant. No offense, taxi drivers.

However, most CPAs have clients making money, don't they? Even clients losing money, and hopefully a few living the American Dream. It's not a reach to assume that the CPA could give us some type of advice about how to make more money and save on taxes.

This is where I started to realize the opportunity and power I had to change people's lives!

Regrettably, for a whole host of reasons, millions of Americans don't turn to a CPA for this critical advice and support.

I'm confident that if many taxpayers would just let their guard down for a moment, they might find their CPA is struggling to tell them something. That is where this story begins.

CONCEPT

1

THE SECRET TO **TAX PLANNING**

THE MEETING

It was a dreary day in March. You know the type of day. It was cold. The flowers had not yet started to bloom. One didn't know if it was about to rain, snow, or just stay cloudy and bleak.

What made the day even more unbearable was it was the day we went to see our accountant. It wasn't a meeting we looked forward to. Sometimes we would talk over the phone, or simply drop off our paperwork. Today, however, we were to "meet."

Any red-blooded American knows what my wife and I were feeling as we walked up to the building. How much were we going to owe in taxes? Would we have the money to pay or would we be lucky enough to get a refund?

In years past I had sometimes taken it upon myself to prepare our own tax returns relying on what claimed to be the most cutting-edge software. But I still always felt I was missing something in the process. Maybe it was a particular deduction or just the lonely feeling of hoping to have someone tell me the tax return was OK.

Nevertheless, this year my wife and I had decided we ought to try *IT* again—that conversation with our CPA. The hope was that a planning meeting would actually help us save on some taxes. Maybe it would even benefit our retirement plans and we would accomplish "wealth building," as some have termed it.

My wife had confided in me on the way there that all she wanted was to simply understand the concepts we discussed in the ominous meeting about to occur. She was embarrassed to admit feeling vulnerable and uneducated when it came to discussions about taxes and our finances. I didn't belittle her or make fun of her. Deep down I felt the same way, but couldn't admit it. I was trying to lead us into the lion's den with as much faith and confidence as I could.

We arrived a few minutes early hoping to become familiar with the surroundings and thus lessen the intimidation we would soon feel. The waiting room was worse than a dentist's office. At least you knew the pain would be over soon with the dentist, but with taxes we assumed we would be paying the bill to Uncle Sam well into the summer. What have they said now? We don't start earning our own income until some time in April? Ironically, it will add insult to injury when tax freedom day finally falls on the filing deadline of April 15th.

The meeting started out as it always had in the past. "Let me see your records," our CPA said. He lowered his glasses, started thumbing through everything—asking a few questions that we thought were insightful, at least for a moment, but the feeling was fleeting. We realized he was just looking for a number to plug into a specific box or place on a line in some forsaken IRS form.

I asked a question about saving some taxes this year, and he immediately brought up the list of itemized deductions. These I was familiar with, but really wondered if they had an impact. He said they did, but who knows? One just answers the questions hoping your CPA will smile and say, "Great! I was hoping you would say that." But he never does.

"Where is the interest statement for your second mortgage?" . . . "Didn't you have some unreimbursed employee expenses at work this year?" he asked my wife. The typical questions simply caused us to regurgitate information, and no real planning was even considered.

Then came the comment from the CPA I most hated, "Well . . . thanks for bringing in your medical expenses, but you phase out because of your income." He usually then chuckles and says, "I'm sorry, you just make too much money." I wonder to myself, it doesn't feel like I make too much money. Why does he say it that way? Damn him.

This time was not like other meetings. No, this time my wife and I had prepared for the upcoming precious moment: THE MOMENT before we get up from the table and he says to come back in three weeks to pick up our tax return.

My wife squeezed my hand under the table, and with as much courage as she could muster, or out of frustration, or just pleading, she asked, "Isn't there something we could do this year to save more in taxes? There has got to be a strategy of some sort."

And then he said it. I actually couldn't believe it. "Well, let's see . . . we could put something in your IRA. You know the limits went up a little this year." I wanted to reach across the table and slap him!

I can't count how many times I had heard this fall-back comment from our CPA. "Let's just contribute to your IRA . . . that will help."

Is that really all I have to look forward to as part of the *planning* process? Couldn't my CPA come up with something better than that?

Suddenly I had the overwhelming feeling I should have just bought another version of the infamous "software" at Costco last month. I could do better than this, and I don't even know anything about taxes. I started to hyperventilate and was torn between yelling or falling back into my chair in complete exasperation.

My wife and I stared at each other wondering where the meeting would go next and hoping it would get better—and fast.

EXITING

I don't know what I was expecting. My CPA was as old as my father. In fact, he was my father's best friend for years. The irony was that we actually felt lucky to be working with him. He had expanded his firm over the years, but instead of having us work with one of his junior CPAs, he had agreed to work with us *personally* because of his relationship with my dad. Truthfully, I wondered if this was a favor or a curse.

Of course, a few years ago I had pressed him a little harder and demanded a different CPA in the office, one that was a little more creative.

This was before I gave preparing my own tax returns a shot. That meeting went even worse.

The CPA was apparently creative, but we couldn't understand a word she said. She was trying to elicit facts and goals from us and promised a plan that we could rely on to save on taxes. She started to explain how the tax code worked; I mean *actually* worked.

My wife left to go to the bathroom during the meeting that year and never came back to the conference room. I found her outside on a park bench drinking a latte from Starbucks and talking with a friend on her cell phone. She had gone into denial or flight . . . or something.

In the conference room I tried to fight it out for as long as I could. At one point I leaned over the table trying to understand her references to the Master Tax Guide, as she quoted chapter and verse. We even sketched out a few ideas, but they didn't make sense to me. I seriously started to daydream about the summer vacation we were planning and forgot she was even talking. So much for a creative approach.

Why is it that CPAs are such poor communicators? It's as if the IRS chooses the students they *want* to go through the accounting programs at college and become the future CPAs. That's it! It's a conspiracy!

If the IRS couldn't confuse us themselves, they would leave it to CPAs to implement the plan of complete apathy and disinterest in tax planning or any hope of any tax savings.

The meeting this year was over. After the IRA comment, I just couldn't muster up any more interest in the conversation. I looked over at my wife. She couldn't even look me in the eye. She was just looking down at the table. I knew she had given up like I had.

To add insult to injury, we had a long walk back to the lobby. The illustrious CPA we inherited from my father was actually a partner and thus we had to meet in the corner office at the end of several turns and hallways. I couldn't take it. I started to feel like I was going to have an anxiety attack and had to get out of there. I told my wife, "To hell with it! I'm just going to call back tomorrow and pick up our information. I can prepare our own taxes better than this."

I grabbed my wife's arm and headed for the nearest stairway exit. It was like a breath of fresh air smelling the cement in the stairwell. I didn't even want to talk. I knew she didn't either. We just started to walk down the stairs in a trance.

I can't remember how many floors we descended before we realized we were at the bottom floor and we weren't actually going to be able to exit directly outdoors. We would have to weave our way through someone else's office.

As we opened the door into a darkened hallway, I quickly realized this unknown office was closed. I knew we needed to hurry and look for an exit to the front of the building. Although I felt like we were trespassing, the last thing I wanted to do was go upstairs and back through our CPA's office.

We turned down the hall, and I realized that we were headed in the right direction and essentially the only way out. Hoping not to see anyone, I was a little nervous when I noticed a light coming out of an office door ahead of us.

My wife looked at me and without saying a word we started to smirk at each other. I whispered, "Do you feel like you are on *America's Most Wanted*?" I loved to see her smile at my dumb jokes. It was my standard protocol to quote a familiar movie whenever possible. This little throwback was from Tim Allen in *Santa Clause*.

As we started to tiptoe down the hall and past the door—as if it would help on carpet—I could hear the people in the office laughing and talking with excited voices. I was immediately confident they wouldn't hear us.

I then heard something that utterly shocked me. A female voice said loudly, "I can't believe how much we are going to save in taxes this year! Why didn't our old CPA tell us this?"

I stopped in my tracks and looked at my wife with wide eyes. I didn't have to say it, but she could read my mind. Did you just hear what I did?

My mind was reeling. We were several steps past the door at this point, but I couldn't bring myself to keep walking down the hall. What do we do? We couldn't just eavesdrop. Awkwardly, we stood there frozen in our steps, and both of us wondered what conversation they could be having that was so powerful.

CONCEPT 1 / **The Secret to Tax Planning**

Wasn't there a movie quote I could pull off the top of my head for my wife that would justify listening in? I couldn't think of anything.

We just tried to listen through the crack in the door.

A LEAP OF FAITH

Well, it seemed longer, but it was probably only a few moments. All of a sudden we could tell the meeting was coming to an end, and it was going to be an odd situation to say the least if we didn't get moving fast.

We started down the hall quickly. We got to the lobby of the office when the door behind us opened and we heard a voice holler out, "Can I help you?" We were stuck. I had to say something.

I turned around and blurted out a few words to the effect that we were coming through from upstairs and were just headed out. "No problem," the voice echoed down the hall. "I thought you were here for my next tax planning appointment."

Almost in unison my wife and I looked at each other with that "I can't believe it look." Our eyes communicated silently, "Should we say something?" I then audibly said to my wife, "Why not?" and smiled. She shrugged her shoulders in agreement, and we turned towards the voice.

As we waited in the lobby area for a moment, the "happy" couple, as I later termed them, emerged from the darkened hallway toward us. They were wrapping up their involved conversation. We exchanged a pleasant glance with the other couple. Then a confident young man said hello to us as he bid the happy couple farewell. I couldn't tell if he was actually young in age, but he certainly was fit and full of energy.

Again he asked if he could assist us in some way. In a tentative voice I explained that when we heard the words "tax planning appointment," we felt we might be interested and asked what he did. He stated in a matter-of-fact sort of way, "I'm a CPA and would love to talk. What's going on?"

I thought this was a little too cavalier and casual for me, and was visibly taken aback. My wife jumped in and said, "Well, we were just upstairs meeting with our CPA, and it didn't go too well. We're a little frustrated."

In an empathetic voice and with tongue in cheek, he said, "Ohhh, one of those meetings, huh? Didn't go too well?" I immediately piped in, "That's an understatement!"

He then popped off and said, "Why is it that CPAs have the hardest time communicating?" He laughed and added, "We don't mean to be. It's just the nature of so many of us. We're just nerds and hate talking. You should see us in a bar trying to pick up a member of the opposite sex. It's not a pretty sight."

My jaw almost dropped to the floor. I was immediately captivated with his self-deprecating humor. I think my wife was beaming, too, and we both shook our heads in agreement.

"It's crazy," he went on. "Taxes are the biggest expense in our lives, but no one wants to talk about them. CPAs think the topic is either too boring and complicated or a conversation isn't going to be helpful anyway. Then to top it all off, you have an industry of practitioners that are introverts and generally don't want to have engaging conversations to complicate the matter."

What planet is this guy from? It was almost sounding too good to be true. I think he could sense I was becoming a little apprehensive, and he quickly interjected, "I'm sorry, I don't mean to beat up CPAs . . . there are many, many great CPAs out there that WANT to talk with their clients. It's just they're hard to find sometimes, and a lot of clients don't help the situation either."

"What do you mean by that?" I asked. He was almost sheepish as he said, "Well, most taxpayers have become accustomed to three bad habits." With his fingers and the animation of an infomercial he said, "First, people don't think that paying their CPA more is actually going to result in savings on taxes. They shop for the cheapest tax return preparation fees like they shop for new tires. Who is going to be the fastest and most inexpensive?

"Second, millions of Americans with their do-it-yourself mentality have started doing their taxes themselves with over-the-counter software. The rationale being that if I can't save taxes, at least I'll save on tax prep fees.

"I think most people deep down know these aren't the wisest approaches to preparing their taxes, but they look at tax services as a commodity and not really helpful. Is that how we want to approach the biggest cost in our lives? I don't think so."

My wife and I concurred, gave a look of encouragement, and nodded for him to go on.

"Finally, many taxpayers think that your tax refund or payment 'is what it is'—that their tax return will be the same no matter who prepares it, unless there's a mistake. When in reality, if you take your tax return to five different CPAs, you will more than likely get five different results. It all depends on the collective risk tolerance of you and your CPA, the creative attitude you share, and the skill set of your CPA."

My wife said that she felt the same way and it made sense. I couldn't disagree either, so I stayed quiet. But I was thinking to myself, "This guy doesn't realize that we oftentimes feel helpless in the situation and don't know where to turn."

I think many of us just want to get our tax returns filed and over with, and then get on with our lives. It's a necessary evil once a year. We just block out any thoughts about tax planning because it is too painful.

Don't get me wrong, I love living in the United States and wouldn't want to live anywhere else. However, like most people, I just operate in denial when it comes to tax planning. Essentially, we're scared to admit that we really don't do tax planning—and feel and believe that. It is what it is.

Was there hope? What was this man saying? Was it a mean joke? I had a thousand thoughts going through my mind at once. Was it worth continuing our conversation? Was this going to turn into a scam, and was he going to offer me some lotion or juice and a chance to join his "downline?" Heaven forbid!

I think he could sense my skepticism, which again flew in the face of CPA communication skills. Could he really be that perceptive to feel the vibes I was sending? Probably not; it was too eerie.

He jumped in at this point and said, "Let me tell you what . . . if you'll sit down for 15 minutes, we'll look at your situation in general, and I'll introduce you to how we operate. Listen, we're a firm that wants you to not only save taxes but also better live the American Dream. We have monthly newsletters, weekly radio shows, and regular live events to help you learn what strategies actually work and which ones are scams. It's up to you. I'll invest a few minutes in you if you will do the same with me."

My wife and I looked at each other fearfully. Not that we would get ripped off or even waste our time, but that we would get let down again. We were like a girl or boyfriend in a bad relationship and just didn't want to get our hearts broken again. At the same time, we had to have hope. Our eyes couldn't lie. We wanted to believe that talking about taxes didn't have to be so miserable.

We shrugged our shoulders in agreement, gathered as much enthusiasm as we could muster, and followed him down the hall to the door with the light on.

TWO WORLDS

As we sat down, we immediately started diving into the facts. Married. Two corporate jobs. Teenage kids and a little one. Homeowners with a reasonable mortgage, which was more reasonable before the last "adjustment" in the real estate market. Pay some money to charity each year. You know . . . the basics.

At almost the exact instant we finished our laundry list of facts, he pulled his chair forward to the edge of his desk and said, "Now I know you're not like *all* Americans. We have clients that are single, retired, married, children, no children, etc. . . . But let me tell you what's going to happen. I'm going to plug the figures you have just given me into your tax return, and you're going to be screwed. I hate to tell you, but in your particular situation I can't help you. You're not giving me anything to work with."

I knew it! My feelings were immediately confirmed. It was too good to be true! No CPA can help us, and he just offended me further by making me walk down the hall to his office with all of his positive talk. It proves again that one can't even hope to talk in a positive manner about taxes.

But then he kept going . . . and with an inquisitive look I was trying to see why he was continuing the conversation after dropping that last bombshell.

"See, we live in a country where two worlds exist. Not the haves and have nots, but those that work for the 'man' and those that work for themselves. I need to ask you, no, beg you, to consider having a small business in your family picture. I'm not asking you to quit your jobs or your careers, but open your mind to some sort of entrepreneurial activities."

I immediately started retreating to my happy place and thought, "But I don't want a small business. At least I don't think I do. I'm too busy, and at the very least I would never think of quitting my corporate career to start a business."

However, he didn't let me dwell on my thoughts too long. He just kept going, and the energy in the room started to elevate dramatically. This guy ACTUALLY believed this stuff! He was so excited I had to put my guard down and give it a chance.

He started emphatically with the statement, "Think of job security. What happens if something goes wrong at work? Do you have an income source to fall back on? What about being in charge of your own project with no boss? The independence and autonomy to take your idea from start to finish can be liberating!"

Then he got my wife's complete attention when he almost shouted, "Consider your teenagers! Have you been wanting to find work for them to earn money? Something productive you might be able to do with them? How about just teaching them a work ethic rather than how to play *Halo 3* on interactive mode with a kid from across the world in Germany? A family project like this could literally change your kids' lives."

Incredulously he started to smirk and said, "What about retirement? Is your 401(k) at work going to be enough? Seriously? Don't even think about Social Security either! Why not try to start SOMETHING on the side that could actually build some long-term wealth or equity?"

"NOT TO MENTION TAX PLANNING! Let's start moving after-tax expenses to above-the-line expenses. What I mean by this is creating legitimate business deductions with expenses you are already paying for. What about your cell phone, your home computer, travel, dining, home office, laptops . . . the list goes on and on."

And almost like a climax in a movie, he looked us in the eyes, and as he peered into my soul, he said, "Why not truly live the American Dream?

"See . . . just having a small business on the side can open up so many opportunities and even benefits beyond tax planning." He pulled out a yellow pad of paper and started frantically writing down the list of ideas he just rattled off. (See Figure 1.1.)

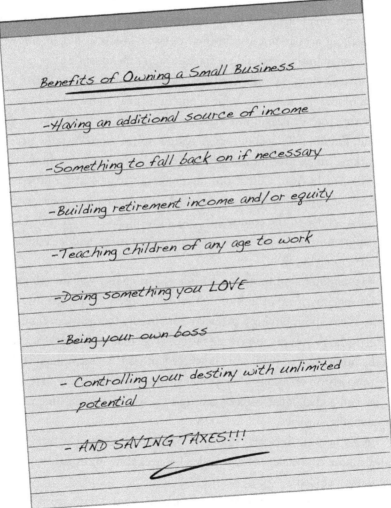

Benefits of Owning a Small Business

- Having an additional source of income

- Something to fall back on if necessary

- Building retirement income and/or equity

- Teaching children of any age to work

- Doing something you LOVE

- Being your own boss

- Controlling your destiny with unlimited potential

- AND SAVING TAXES!!!

Figure 1.1

"Again, I'm not saying quit your job if you love it. But at least consider the possibility of turning your hobby or passion into a business and creating income and wealth in the process. Legitimately."

The stillness in the room was tangible. He looked at us as we soaked it all in. We just sat there pondering. I felt like I had just gotten blindsided with a mental left hook I didn't see coming. I needed to digest this. I could see my wife was reeling, too, and gazing at nothing in particular. Not frustrated or confused, but just pondering the ideas.

Own a small business! This is totally not our style. It's too risky. This is something my harebrained brother- or sister-in-law would do. But what kind of small business would we start? It didn't make sense!

I love my corporate job. Well, maybe not love it. But that's what I went to school for. Not to mention for a long time. I can't give up on that.

Before the silence got awkward, he piped in. "Just a thought . . . hear me out. I'm not talking about opening up a donut shop down the street or embarking on an invention that you have to patent or get manufactured and shipped in from China. I'm talking about maybe just a little rental property. Maybe a product or idea that you could simply sell on eBay. Maybe a service in the community like mowing lawns with your kids or recycling projects. Think of something you love to do, and let's think of a business model to fit it!"

He couldn't stop throwing out ideas. His energy was infectious. "As you're soaking this in, think of that rental property idea I just threw out there. What about buying a property here locally that you can fix up as a family? Maybe you get something farther away that could work as a rental in the hometown of your parents where you visit. You can then work on the property on vacations when you have to see family anyway." He looked at me and added, "Just think of getting a tax write-off every time you visit your mother-in-law!"

Now he went too far. He could really make my visit with my wife's family more enjoyable? My wife rolled her eyes knowing exactly what I was thinking. I smiled.

Once more, he let the moment sink in. He slid back from his desk and just smiled with excitement. Like he had just laid out an assortment of candy for some kids, and we were supposed to be excited to choose several pieces.

However, we just sat there looking down and nodding our heads. We weren't beat up or frustrated. Just thinking.

We had asked for some ideas, and we certainly got some. But this may have been too much. I didn't want to change my lifestyle or habits. I just wanted to save on taxes. All of a sudden I started to feel like a candidate for the *Biggest Loser*. Can't I lose weight by just taking a pill? Can't I save on taxes by just checking a box or something?

I didn't know what to think.

The one thing I was most surprised about was how this tax-savings thing could impact so many other areas of my life. Teaching my kids? Building wealth? Living the American Dream? It sounded too good to be true . . . again. I was already starting to have more doubts about this concept. Maybe the greatest doubt I was having now was if I had the time to make it work.

The man then said in a very understanding and empathetic tone, something again uncharacteristic of our other CPA, "Let me give you some homework. Please go home, and think about this conversation. Consider some entrepreneurial ideas. See if you could envision yourself owning at least some investment real estate or starting a small service or product-based business. Basically, doing something *different* than you are now. Please do that for me.

"Obviously, you can't expect a different result without making some changes in your life. I'm sorry I don't have a magic wand."

Then as if we were high-fiving after a Monday night football game, he said, "If you feel like I can be your guy for tax planning, please call my assistant and set up a retainer and a planning appointment. She'll give you a list of things to bring in, or we can simply start talking about your ideas and plans for this year and many more to come."

Was it really going to be that soft of a sale?

Then my wife blurted out without any warning, at least to me, "Well, what type of stuff would be a write-off if we started a small business?" Then she started rattling off items that she just bought at Staples and Home Depot.

Like a protective father he simply smiled and said, "Slow down, tiger. We'll talk about that in our next appointment."

She was visibly frustrated with his answer, but then we looked at each other and quickly realized we had a lot to talk *and* think about.

His final words were poignant. As I look backed at that meeting, it truly gave me the basic guidance I needed for many months to come. "This isn't all about small business. I have other strategies or concepts that will literally change your financial picture and save on taxes at the same time, but having a small business and/or rental property is a significant part of the equation."

Continuing, he emphasized with emotion, "Please be patient, and give this first concept a chance. All the rest will come together like a beautifully woven tapestry over time. Remember, your stitching may look a little different than that of your family and friends. Everyone's plans are a little different and come together on different timetables. Let's dive into yours, and help you to start living your *Dream*."

SUMMARY
The Secret to Tax Planning

Having a small business or real estate investment of some sort has to be a major consideration if we want to save on taxes. This is the Secret that corporate America completely disregards and marginalizes! Moreover, tax planning can be exciting and actually enjoyable. It doesn't have to be miserable. However, we have to realize that saving on taxes requires a significant mental shift.

Some say it is too risky to have a small business—and more than likely a waste of time. I completely disagree and argue that it is actually more risky not to have a small business. Certainly there can be risk, but it can be mitigated. The benefits are truly phenomenal.

Now, let me be clear, this doesn't mean quitting your job or firing your stockbroker! It just means having at least something on the side and trying to live outside of the box to some degree. Don't just work solely for the "Man."

Those who really want to save on taxes, have some financial security to fall back on, and work toward their own retirement plan, just to name a few goals, must consider small-business ownership as well as rental real estate.

Finally, it doesn't mean taking risks. I believe you are actually reducing your risks if you approach small business in the right way. Why not have a project brewing on the side or build equity in something to help supplement your retirement plan? Don't give up on this concept. Be open to it. You're creating options! We need options. This is truly where real tax planning and the American Dream begin.

2

A NEW
PERSPECTIVE

THE TEMPTATION

My wife and I didn't talk as much as I thought we would after the mysterious meeting with the "new CPA," as we now referred to him. He wasn't ours yet . . . just the "'new one." The next few days seemed to fly by as usual. We were back to our normal routine.

You know how things go. You just get busy. Married couples don't talk as much as single people think. Well, maybe they already know that.

The reality was that we didn't talk much because we really didn't know what to talk about. It quickly became apparent that it was a lot easier to talk about starting a business than actually doing it.

It was embarrassing to some degree. My wife and I were educated, at least college educated, and had some great work experience to boast about. But starting a business took a whole new set of tools.

We now understood how important it was to have practical guidance through the process, so we didn't waste our time and, better yet, didn't lose our shirts.

With a mild sense of intrigue, as well as a little hope, I was looking forward to the weekend to boost my spirits. My younger brother was coming over. He was in his late 20s, single, and living large, as we married men in our 40s would say. He was dating and traveling a little, and with no strings attached. However, what interested me the most now was having some time to talk about his small-business ventures.

Immediately after high school he had started college, but he always had some sort of small-business project going on the side. In fact, it wasn't long after starting college that he decided to become a chiropractor.

I loved to tease him and ask when he was going to become a "real doctor." He didn't like my jokes, especially after I came to him for regular adjustments when I started having back problems a few years ago. He was a miracle worker with my overall health and that of others. His business was thriving because other patients felt the same way. I called them "clients," and he hated that. Oh well, that's what big brothers are for.

Interestingly, not long ago when he said he was buying a little rental property, I rolled my eyes and thought it was just another one of his impulsive schemes. However, after our recent meeting with the CPA, I had really changed my opinion of my brother, and at least to some degree, felt that I better understood his deep-seated desire to get out and live his entrepreneurial dreams.

But again, the irony moved in like a set of storm clouds. As usual, destiny seems to play its normal part in all our lives. Instead of an exhilarating conversation about small business and feeding off of his energy, something my wife and I were hoping for, we ended up discussing the struggles he was having with his latest project.

Sales were down, costs were up, and, of course, stress was at an all-time high. He admitted to some mistakes this last go-around. He thought this last economic boom would never end, or at least only taper off rather than crash. It was something a lot of other people believed, too.

There were lessons to be learned, of course, but my wife and I probably shot each other a hundred looks as we were talking with him between the barbecue and watching a game of something on ESPN. Each look seemed to say, "Are we seriously going to consider this type of risk in our lives?"

To make matters even more precarious, he mentioned one of his rental properties was going into foreclosure. It had negative cash flow and was causing serious financial worries for him. However, it was interesting that he didn't mention his other two quality rental properties that were doing well. I had to pry that out of him as I searched for a glimmer of hope in his small-business ventures.

Nevertheless, it was like a shot across the bow of our ship. We had already turned our sails in the direction of entrepreneurship, even if it was just a mental shift. We certainly hadn't taken any substantive action yet, but we were definitely interested, if not already emotionally committed.

The one offshoot of our conversation that was very surprising was the discussion about our newly discovered CPA. My brother was fascinated about our experience and kept asking questions about what we had learned. I thought he had all of this tax stuff dialed in. He was supposed to be taking advantage of all of the small-business tax write-offs and living the Dream!

However, come to find out he was longing for a relationship with a planning CPA as much as we were. He complained about his regular experience of having to bring ideas to his CPA, rather than his CPA giving him strategies to implement. Apparently, small-business skills and tax strategies just don't fall in your lap when you decide to become an entrepreneur.

It was interesting to discover that many professionals in medicine, construction, and sales, just to name a few, consistently struggle trying to balance running their business and being skilled in their profession. My brother made me commit to keeping him posted on any further developments with this new CPA.

Anyway, I had expected a more motivating talk with my brother and now was feeling more dubious about this whole entrepreneurial thing.

With the seeds of hope, before the weekend we had called the new CPA and made an appointment to do some tax planning. I was now regretting we had made the call. I had a feeling we may have been too impetuous and were moving too quickly. Fear was setting in.

As Sunday evening came to an end and the busy workweek was upon us again, my wife found a quiet moment to ask me my thoughts.

Of course I shrugged and said I didn't know what to do. I really felt we were onto something. Savings on taxes was, of course, the original priority, and it seemed we were actually onto something bigger than that. But then, maybe we weren't.

One might think that the obvious temptation was to jump in with both feet, and better live and experience the American Dream—or at least enhance it. Regrettably, the immediate temptation was to stay the course and do nothing. And the temptation was strong. Both my wife and I really felt that something was trying to keep us from pursuing our dream of bettering ourselves.

However, when I slowed down and really pondered things, I felt that the right thing to do was to pursue this concept of entrepreneurship. My wife agreed. It was an incredible feeling to have this experience with her. We were both on the same page. It pulled us together.

The bonding with my wife also reminded me of something my brother said earlier that weekend. He explained that although he hadn't yet found Mrs. Right, his entrepreneurial passion was a huge part of his identity and enhanced his relationships with his friends and the women he dated. It kept him positive, hopeful, and anxious to wake up and fight his battles each day.

All of this feel-good talk aside, one of the hurdles that seemed to keep slapping me in the face was I didn't even know what kind of business I wanted to start. How could I be thinking about entrepreneurism and small business without an interest in any particular business or moneymaking concept? My wife confided in me that she felt the same way. We both started to fall into a state of apathy.

We couldn't seem to get our engine started, for lack of a better analogy, and frankly we didn't know how. The fear of the unknown was paralyzing. We just operated on autopilot the next few days and almost gave into the temptation to quit before we even got started. Several times we talked about calling and cancelling the appointment with the CPA.

It was a precarious time.

A VISION

This frustration of trying to find my calling, or simply that perfect small business, was mounting. I knew I needed to get started doing something, but what that something was seemed very elusive.

Then an interesting thing happened. I was driving home from work on a day when everything seemed a little burdensome. Not a bad day. Just a hard day. The type of workday you hope to have only once a week. The type of day your employer wishes you had five days a week. The extremely productive days, I suppose.

As I turned a familiar corner on my commute home, I saw a little house with a For Sale sign in front of it. I had driven down this road hundreds of times before and had never really noticed the house, but it just jumped out at me this time.

I was attracted to it almost magnetically. I didn't know why. The only time I've looked for these signs before was when we bought our home a few years back. But I couldn't take my eyes off of the house as I drove by.

I found myself unconsciously making a U-turn and pulling up across the street to check it out. It was a nice little house, but something I would never buy to live in. It just wasn't my style.

But I could hear the words from the new CPA echoing in my mind, "Have you ever considered a rental property?"

Maybe this could really work. Could I actually be looking at my own rental?

I walked up to the house. The flier in the little box on the sign started out "A great starter home or rental property." I just looked up, staring at nothing but the sky, and realized that the local community college was just two blocks away.

My mind was spinning. The adrenalin was flowing. Is this what the American Dream feels like, or is this what a client of Bernie Madoff felt like before he wrote a check? I was confused. I needed to clear my mind. I drove the rest of the way home with the windows down.

As I walked slowly up to the front steps of our house, I experienced another unexpected event. My wife met me at the door with a magazine article and started talking quickly without taking a visible pause to breathe. I didn't know if I should cut her off or just let her keep going. Like a smart husband married for more than three years, I shut up and let her keep talking.

My wife has always been a driven woman. When we met in college, she had career plans, and graduating from college was just one of the stepping stones to get what she wanted.

When she started her first corporate job, she was amazing! They loved her, and she, of course, moved quickly up the ladder in her department. But then it happened. The unexpected, yet expected, bundle of joy. We knew we wanted children and that part was expected, but she didn't anticipate motherhood being so satisfying. It clearly competed with her career ambitions. She thought she could easily go back to work and do the day-care thing in perpetuity. She was wrong.

Now we have three great kids. She's been a phenomenal mom, but she also wanted to keep her skills useful. Frankly, we could also use the money. So currently she has a part-time job with a company where her training and education is an asset, and remarkably she has found a good balance between the two responsibilities.

But she also had an interesting experience the same day I ran across the rental. She was at work and her supervisor asked her to send a gift basket to one of their important clients. Something unique, not too expensive, but definitely tasteful.

At least these were the bits and pieces I was gathering from her frantic dialogue as she was talking faster than Nancy Grace on a tirade.

Apparently she couldn't find an acceptable gift basket for the client. Then she made her point, "You know, I could totally start a business creating gift baskets tailored to the types of clients we have at work." She was then silent, and the thought hung out there as if I could touch it. "Start a gift basket business? Are you serious? I thought we were going to talk about this?" Of course, she immediately retorted, "We did talk about it . . . at the new CPA's office."

Every husband knows what just happened. I started to have visions of wearing an apron or chef hat with the logo of the new business prominently printed on the front. Of course these marketing pieces would be displayed openly for all of my friends to see and mock me. My fear of small business immediately shifted to the fear of this business. No offense to gift basket makers. It's just not what I had in mind as my next career.

I went through my normal conservative and cautious arguments with her. I pointed out the time this venture of hers would take from her other responsibilities and also the capital it might take to get it off the ground. She had an answer for every one of my concerns.

After a fairly engaging debate as we tried to make some food for the kids, I decided I would throw out my little bombshell, too.

With a smirk on my face, I said tentatively, "I also have something I want to bring into the mix. I saw this little house on my drive home." And rather than say the word "rental," I handed her the description of the property while I made my pitch.

Well, needless to say, I think the words "calling the kettle black," "are you serious," and "this is a lot more than a few gift baskets" were floated through the kitchen.

It was an interesting evening as we watched a little television and talked between our normal chores and duties with homework. Doing fifth grade math that night didn't help me feel any more confident either.

The upcoming meeting with the CPA started to seem more like a necessity than one of curiosity or passing interest. We needed a referee, mediator, coach, and teacher all in one. I was skeptical.

ELIMINATING FEAR

We walked into the appointment with trepidation, but still with a slight feeling of excitement. We didn't know what to expect, but it felt right to go, and we needed some direction on these new business ideas.

After a cordial greeting, the first question out of our CPA's mouth was, "So what do you think of entrepreneurship?" We knew the question was coming, but we were still unsure how to answer.

My wife took control of the discussion immediately and said we were open to entrepreneurship but had concerns. She wasn't lying. We had been talking over the idea for the past few days. Going over the pros and cons. What the possibilities could be. What the risks were. Could we come up with the right business idea and make it work. Numerous concerns to say the least. However, it always came back to the same issue.

My wife got the discussion started. "My husband and I just keep saying to each other, we don't know where to get started on this whole process, and frankly we don't feel we have the education or experience to pull off a small business right now." She blurted it out, and as I looked at the CPA, my eyes showed my agreement without saying a word.

I don't think we were embarrassed; we were just being honest. Heck, we had college educations—great educations from great schools. I was in middle management on the fast track to executive level, as some would term it. My wife would have made it to that level already if it wasn't for the kids, which again were a blessing.

But I knew we weren't alone. My brother the chiropractor said he felt inadequate to give us direction on the first steps to take, and he had been an entrepreneur his whole life. He felt he was constantly shooting from the hip and was anxious to hear what the CPA had to say today as well.

The CPA was just sitting back listening to us intently, and I could actually sense some level of empathy. Then without warning but with confidence and reassurance, he began telling us a little about his journey as a professional. He reminded us that believe it or not, when you graduate as a CPA, you don't come out of school either with the practical skills to run a small business or the ability to advise others on the process.

He told us that it had taken him years of continuing education classes, learning from seasoned and business-minded CPAs, as well as watching the success and failures of countless clients. Leaning across the table and with the concern of a religious counselor, he said, "Your concerns about how and what to do are completely valid. I certainly don't expect you to take on something you're not ready to."

As we discussed the topic, we discovered that many entrepreneurs consistently struggle with the basics of how to keep good records, save on taxes, protect their assets, and build wealth all at the same time. They have the constant battle of trying to juggle all of these responsibilities and keep balance in their life.

In the end, the reality is that running a business takes skills that many of us don't learn in college, let alone high school or from our parents. My wife and I were feeling the void that many business owners and wannabe entrepreneurs face every day.

He continued, "We all just need to remember that sometimes the best advice a person can receive when starting down the entrepreneur path is to take baby steps. But guess what? I think I can give you a set of keys today and some advice that will help you start that car of yours and get you driving down the road."

Again, we were shocked at how perceptive he could be as well as empathetic. I knew we were in the right place at the right time.

At this point we were extremely eager to hear what this key to get our business off and running was. My wife even blurted out, "So what is it we need to do at this point?"

First he had a big grin on his face. Then narrowing his lips and focus, he said, "It's the same key for those already in business and those just beginning. You have to hunger and thirst for education. I know this sounds like a cliché, but it's true. In fact, some hate to have this be an ongoing requisite in their business, but it's critical."

He went on to explain how reading good books, listening to audio lectures, grabbing up DVDs, and catching live presentations whenever and wherever we could was a must.

He emphasized, "Education will ultimately eliminate the fear, misunderstanding, and frustration small-business owners face every day. Moreover, it will certainly increase profits and opportunities. Too many small-business owners give up on education when they start their business."

I understood now why my brother was so interested in our relationship with this new CPA. I realized that one of the main reasons he had been successful with his previous small-business ventures was his voracious appetite for learning.

Just because he started to experience a little success or had a crisis didn't mean he put off learning until he had more time. He was constantly trying to soak up as much information as he could.

When our new advisor said all this, I knew he was right. It was simple. Maybe it wasn't necessary to say, but in reality I'm glad he said it.

"Listen," he said, "I'm not going anywhere. I have online videos, a weekly radio show, and regular speaking events. Also, don't forget we're a team around here, and we want to be a support to you in your ventures for years. We have a monthly e-newsletter, a monthly live video broadcast, and a powerful website. We hope that we are constantly sharing information with you that will help you on your quest."

Right then and there, I looked at my wife and squeezed her hand. She looked in my eyes, too, and we both knew we were headed in the right direction. The fear was slowly leaving, but the practical steps for tomorrow were still looming.

PATIENCE

Putting this "education" concept to the test, I was hoping he had a plan for us. "So now what?" I asked with a little skepticism. "What can we start doing this week?"

He confidently smiled and said, "I have two things I want you to begin working on. Starting this week, I want you to be on the hunt," he exclaimed, hitting his fist on the table.

"I want you to start brainstorming ideas on a regular basis on what type of business project fits you and your family best. Maybe it's one or two or even more concepts you start to develop." He encouraged us to start writing down ideas. "I am so excited for you," he said.

My wife and I looked at each other and simultaneously said "white-boarding," and laughed a little that we both thought of the same words. We were, of course, familiar with this process from the corporate world. Brainstorming in work groups is a constant procedure and important process in business.

We weren't stupid. We were obviously already doing this and at the least making mental notes of ideas and projects. My wife was already scoping out products for her gift baskets, and I had driven by that little rental property for sale a handful of times just to envision what I might do with it.

However, he cautioned us not to jump on the first idea we came up with and told us we should go through hundreds of ideas or pieces of real estate before finding the right one; even if we eventually went back to one we saw or thought of in the beginning.

My wife and I agreed with him as we discussed the concept. We recognized the importance of just getting familiar with the profit model of different small-business projects and how different real estate deals might play out. The last thing our CPA wanted us to do was to rush into a deal.

He committed us to start reading entrepreneurial magazines and articles, listening to his radio shows and videos, and reading his newsletters. Basically, start soaking in all we could about this other world.

One of the key points he made was the importance of seeking out the right education programs, ones that teach real methods and techniques, not ones that are rah-rah sessions at a convention center where the big answer is "positive attitude" or "determination." Not that those are bad in and of themselves.

I was glad he was emphasizing "real" education. My wife and I are smart, yet we understood we still have a lot more to learn. He said he would guide us through some good educational systems.

Then he leaned forward to emphasize his next point. "The important thing to remember in this process, and I mean process, is that learning how to be a small-business owner or real estate investor takes time," he explained. "You couldn't have started in your current position at your company after one year of college, could you? It's the same here. Don't think one weekend class or one CD set is going to prevent you from making a mistake. Please don't give up on your education."

He continued, "It's also important not to get sucked into the concept that starting a small business or buying real estate is a quick fix to solve your financial woes or a get-rich-quick scheme. Don't let anyone fool you into that mentality. This is going to take a lot of work.

"Moreover, implementing a tax-savings plan is a long-term proposition. I don't want you to start any small-business venture until you feel confident in your heart and mind that your choice is a good project for you."

At this point my wife sheepishly leaned forward and said, "Well, we kinda have a few ideas we were already thinking of pursuing." We knew we were busted. Just a few minutes ago we were talking of concerns and walking out the door; now we had ideas.

He grinned from ear to ear, and without calling us out, he immediately wanted to hear about them. He loved entrepreneurship. I could feel it.

Why is it that our old CPA would have cringed at the idea of a small business? I was starting to realize there are really two types of CPAs out there. Those that want to drop in your W-2 and itemized deductions on your tax return and avoid a real planning meeting vs. those that truly want to find a way to save on taxes, enjoy some creativity, and don't have a problem helping their client create a small-business operation.

After some fun debate back and forth on the ideas, potential benefits, risks, and timelines, the energy level was off the chart. I really felt we were talking about changes in our lives that would have a real lasting impact, if not immediate impact. For one, I could see I was actually going to be a little happier each day and excited to get to the end of the workday. Life was changing, and for the better.

Then almost as if on cue, there was a noticeable pause, and he knew we were ready for the next to-do item. He said, "Now let's get to some real meat and potatoes. There are a few things I want to cover today that will really set the tone for your new business."

I liked the business coaching rah-rah-rah session of ideas; however, I realized we needed to get to work. This was the accountant in him speaking now, and I really appreciated it. Still, I was nervous.

TRACKING THE LITTLE THINGS

Rubbing his hands together, our new CPA exclaimed, "The topic I've been anxious to bring up is bookkeeping," and with a comical grin and raised eyebrows, he emphasized the words "This is when the fun begins!"

With some apprehension I thought to myself, "I don't think I've ever heard a CPA say the words 'fun' and 'bookkeeping' in the same sentence." I actually felt like I was going to be sick. Bookkeeping. You've got to be kidding me. He's going to waste our valuable time on this topic?

Then he reassured us he wasn't crazy and said, "Seriously, this is where tax savings start and your business plans begin. Literally. In fact, you're actually already saving money right now! You are officially in startup mode.

"Your mileage over to the office today, your dining expenses tonight sketching down your ideas," and he conveniently added, "even your accounting fees are no longer tax preparation fees, these are planning fees for your business." My wife and I exchanged glances without saying a word that we liked this feeling. We were starting to save on taxes.

He went on to explain that many small-business owners don't realize how important good record keeping is. Nor do they realize how many expenses could actually be tax deductible.

Therefore, he wanted us to keep track of all of our expenses that were even remotely related to any of our ideas or projects. We were supposed to write them down somewhere and keep a schedule of expenses. He was clear that we didn't need to buy any accounting software yet, we could simply keep a file of receipts or an Excel® spreadsheet of cash or credit card expenses.

Then with an obvious cautious and serious tone, he said, "At the end of the year, we'll go through your expenses and determine which ones can be legitimately written off. Everything has to be accounted for at the end of the year. Don't forget this."

I thought of my brother who was already in business. He seemed to leave the bookkeeping for the end of the year, and the books were always a mess. The CPA explained this is a common problem among entrepreneurs and inevitably means deductions are lost, tax preparation fees are more, and the risk of an audit is higher.

He continued, "Let me explain this startup phase of your business. It is important you understand this concept. The IRS doesn't consider you actually in business until you sell that first cup of lemonade. In fact, let's use a lemonade stand as an example.

"When you are preparing for your new venture, buying lemonade and sugar, getting ice, making your sign, choosing your location, etc., you are in the startup mode. The IRS has determined that you are actually not in business until you sell at least one cup of lemonade.

"Now don't worry. You'll get to deduct those expenses you incurred getting your stand open! I want you to keep track of them, but you'll ultimately deduct them as a startup expense. Thus, that is why it's so important to keep careful track of your expenses."

He was also clear that you can't be in the perpetual state of starting a business. You actually have to start creating revenue or else the IRS will start calling your business a "hobby" and limit your deductions. Then, with a grin and the promise of future excitement and high-fives to come, he exclaimed, "However, in real estate investment there are different rules and hobby loss rules don't apply with a rental property. Wait until you hear one of the best strategies in tax planning!"

Most importantly, he said that he didn't want us to set up a business just to lose money either. That certainly doesn't make good financial sense. I agreed. We are starting a business to make money, and we want to convert as many previously personal expenses to business expenses as possible because that is where the savings are really reaped. More income from a business venture, at a lower tax rate.

In sum, he emphasized that we didn't have to show profit, just revenue to show the IRS we were actually in business.

At this point the energy level was again cranking up, and I realized we were still talking about bookkeeping. I was stunned! It's funny how tax strategies have such a practical application, but we tend to ignore them out of fear of boredom.

I then thought this was a great time to ask the question I had been dying to bring up. "So what is actually a tax write-off? I hear everybody say, 'Oh, that's a tax write-off.' But where do I get the list of write-offs?"

He seemed almost apologetic and said with a sigh, "Well, I wish there was a simple list setting forth what was deductible or not, but according to the IRS Code, it's essentially 'any expense incurred in the production of income.' From there the pages of the tax code grow exponentially."

At this point, he gave us an important juicy nugget of advice.

"Don't worry about what's deductible right now. If you think it is related to the startup of your business or the current operations, keep track of it! Write it down. Make it a game. Try to come up with any possible way an expense could relate to your business so we can try to write it off. Remember, it's the little things that make the biggest difference in the end."

And then he reemphasized, "Just keep track of your expenses. At the end of the year we'll go over them and figure out what is legitimate and what isn't. As the years go on, you'll learn what deductions will work and which ones won't."

For my wife, this simple advice was nice, and she could almost live with it—almost. But she was bordering on incredulous with her tone when she remarked, "But shouldn't we be using some sort of software like Quicken®?"

He smiled ear-to-ear and immediately retorted, "I love it!" In fact, he almost jumped out of his seat. It was as if I had announced to my son we just purchased the most recent version of Xbox®.

"Yes, I would love you to eventually use that type of software. But don't feel you have to rush out and buy a copy this weekend. Keep in mind that Quicken is more for your home finances and QuickBooks® is for your business. There are all sorts of versions, even an online version. Bottom line, you'll certainly want to get some sort of QuickBooks system in place when things start ramping up."

I was almost as excited to start doing bookkeeping as I was listening to his quick facts delivered with such enthusiasm. Well, almost. I'll probably leave that exciting task to my wife, who was already taking notes and shopping for the most recent version on her iPhone®.

Damn that iPhone. I, of course, was a BlackBerry® user. It was a constant debate as to who was more effective. Oh, well.

He then summarized a couple major points. First, he said, it's typical that even with good software, we will often have expenses that don't fall into the system we establish. "Don't get frustrated by this. Just embrace the chaos!" he said.

"Just realize you might pay for something with cash or with a credit card. Also, from time to time you might buy something with your personal account by mistake or in a crisis because you left the business checkbook at home. Just have a spot to track these things in a file."

Second, he suggested that we learn more about QuickBooks. Through his company we can get some entrepreneurial training. We can try a class at his accounting office, an online tutorial, or even just practice with the software itself. As soon as we are ready to open a business bank account and gear up for sales, we can then get QuickBooks cranking.

At this point we were just about on information overload, but we were also still sitting on the edge of our seats. We were coming up with a plan! I wasn't quitting my job, but I was now building something for myself, not my employer.

After giving us a handout titled "Bookkeeping Basics," a copy of which I have included for you at the end of my story (see Appendix A), he ushered us out of the office.

I think he had done this before and knew we couldn't build Rome in a day. But with that said, I knew we had the basic building blocks to start organizing our books and begin some education.

As far as I was concerned, it was mission accomplished. I was brainstorming ideas, soaking up as much education as I could, and keeping track of expenses along the way. Life was going to change, and taxes were going to go down.

SUMMARY
A New Perspective

Getting started in entrepreneurship is actually easier than people think. We just don't know where to turn to get the basic building blocks and learn the steps to take.

In fact, some of you may have fallen into small business by accident. You may have learned a trade or skill that unexpectedly thrust you into entrepreneurship. There are all sorts of professionals who have to wear two hats: knowing their trade and also how to run a business.

Although today's traditional educational tracks don't teach entrepreneurial skills, there's still hope. With some tailored entrepreneurship education and a little commitment to organizational skills, fear, and frustration can disappear.

Some of you have had a small business for years, some are still trying to figure out what small business or real estate project is best for you, even while reading this book. Here are some suggestions and first steps you can take:

- *Strive to do what you love.* If you're going to be in business, choose something you're passionate about.

- *Regularly search for ideas and projects.* What may be a good business fit for you? Also, always be on the lookout for a good real estate deal or rental property.

- *Soak up all the entrepreneurial education you can.* Try to avoid the school of hard knocks. Classes, books, and seminars are a must. Your CPA and team of professionals should be a major resource in this area, and if they aren't, get new ones.

- *Keep good records.* List all of your expenses when starting out. You'll implement and learn the proper bookkeeping skills when the time is right.

See Additional A at the end of this book for an explanation of Bookkeeping Basics that will save you time and money.

CONCEPT

3

FOUNDATIONS

REAL FRIENDS

We were walking out the door with the CPA when things got a lot more precarious. He brought up the word "structure." I thought he meant incorporating or not. Apparently it meant much more than that.

"This weekend I'm speaking at an entrepreneurial event," he announced, unabashed. Without even letting us start to come up with an excuse, he pushed, saying, "This will be a great opportunity for you to start your education and also network with other business owners and investors.

"You don't want to keep paying me per hour for every piece of the puzzle, do you?" He was right, but now I had to sit in one of those damn "seminars." No way!

Up to this point, our plans had been between my wife and me, and our new CPA. But now we were going to have to go "public" as small-business owners? I was only comfortable being secretive about this new part of my life and wasn't ready to tell others, let alone be around other small-business owners. These were the people we made fun of in the corporate machine. Now he wanted me to come out of the closet? I was sick to my stomach.

A co-worker at my office was going to have a heyday with this! You know the guy I'm talking about: the water cooler guy. Everything is fair game at the water cooler, and no one walks away from the watering hole without a dig or sarcastic remark regarding a thing like this.

Moreover, nothing was secret with this friend of mine at the office. We always talk about our plans for the weekend, and he knows when I'm lying. We were good friends, and I valued our friendship. But this was uncharted territory. The expression "coming out of the closet" really hit home now.

While I was still reeling thinking about our new CPA's invitation, I glanced at my wife. I could see she was doing what we all do—trying to figure out what her friends would think.

She was playing out the same nightmare in her mind. How would she tell her friends she was spending her Saturday to go sit in a "guru seminar"? That is what they would call it, or a whole host of other things. Would her friends think we were going broke, or one of us was losing our job?

Why would we go to the other side of the fence and sit in a class with small-business owners? We were corporate folks. We knew better. We were smarter. We had college degrees. At least we had convinced ourselves of this. We knew no real small-business owner had a college degree. They must have dropped out or couldn't get a job.

At the same time I was thinking of excuses. Why was I feeling so self-righteous? My brother told me that if my new CPA had any sort of class or event, he wanted to come. My brother was a professional as well as a business owner, and wouldn't think twice about blowing a Saturday to learn something new. However, he wasn't like all business owners. He was unique, and I knew it.

Why can't small-business owners go to a seminar or conference designed specifically around tax or business planning without seeing one or two eyebrows raised by acquaintances?

Moreover, why do small-business owners think they are too smart to stay current with new laws and strategies? It seems the only acceptable conferences are the ones improving your trade or expertise, not on small-business strategies. Regrettably, doctors go to continuing education courses to be better doctors, not better business owners. They have to rely on sometimes overpriced consultants to run their businesses.

Time had passed in the conversation, but I couldn't tell how long. The CPA knew what to say, "Listen, I realize it is a big decision to start down this small-business path. And again, no one is asking you to quit your jobs. Just come out and see what it's like in this other world. You can have both, you know, but your image as a corporate executive might have to change a little."

Then with a smile he said, "Hey, you could call yourself a venture capitalist or a budding investor. Maybe that would work!"

We both smirked and let out a big sigh. We knew at that point that we would have to come to grips with our public image to some degree, or at least our self-image. Change sucks, but deep down we both knew we were on to something and couldn't contain our enthusiasm.

Soon we would find who our real friends were and who would provide that support structure.

ENCOURAGEMENT

It's mesmerizing to me that when we take steps to better ourselves, it is oftentimes viewed with disdain by our friends. Not to mention our family. You know what I'm saying.

Shouldn't these be the people that encourage you the most? Maybe they really do feel threatened by your efforts and believe it reflects on their own lack of self-esteem or inability to motivate themselves to do better. It's as if they want to bring you down to stay comfortable themselves.

We had decided that we were serious. However, we couldn't commit to a full day seminar on Saturday. Any parent with adolescent children knows that the soccer and Little League associations were first formed to help children experience team sports, but a close second was to ruin every Saturday or Sunday during the prime of their parents' lives.

Sitting on a lawn chair, eating sunflower seeds, and watching your kids pick dandelions while the sporting event takes place around them on the field is the calling of the modern parent.

Although we could only commit a couple of hours to our CPA and the upcoming Saturday seminar, it sure caused some discussion during the week.

At the office I decided to tackle it head-on. I would just tell my co-worker what I was doing when he asked. He could live with it, right? He would just nod his head and say "interesting," and move on to the spread for the most interesting game playing that weekend. Not the case.

As soon as I nonchalantly mentioned to another person in the office what my wife and I were doing between trips to the soccer fields, eyebrows were raised, eyes widened, and questions ensued. I actually had a staff member ask if there were problems with the company and if he should be looking for another job!

After assuring him that everything was fine with the company and our personal finances, I started to share my excitement about small business, investing, and, I venture to say, "you know, the American Dream stuff." That statement didn't even float in the air a second. It fell like a lead balloon.

They thought they were living the Dream. What was I looking for, they demanded? They didn't know what they were missing, and didn't want to know. They were comfortable.

I wasn't comfortable. I wasn't happy knowing my retirement depended on my company matching my 401(k) contributions. I wasn't comfortable having no serious safety net or something to fall back on if my day job was threatened.

Now I was jumping out of bed in the morning thinking of opportunities and ideas. It was nuts!

Meanwhile, my wife took the more politically savvy approach to spreading the news about our plans to her circle of friends: don't say a word unless they pry it out of you. This usually works best with her girlfriends in an effort to keep the rumor mill to a minimum around the neighborhood.

Her approach lasted until about midweek when she was at a school function with one of the kids and talk turned to the weekend's activities. Plans were being made for various excursions on Saturday and carpooling for kids to games. My wife had to mention the "class" as she termed it.

Her friends immediately thought she was going back to the local university for classes. My wife could only let that assumption float for a few exchanges before disclosing it was more of a training seminar.

Most of her friends gave words of encouragement and expressions of astonishment that we needed to find another source of income. They thought we were getting by, if not doing well.

When she explained that we were doing better financially than ever but felt we needed something more, and not just income, they were intrigued at first. "What is it that you want more of they asked?"

This was a little harder to explain.

She didn't focus on retirement goals, which I tended to use as my primary excuse at work, but explained that she really wanted something for us to do with the kids. Something that would teach them a work ethic and the belief that they could own their own business someday.

"We aren't giving up on the kids going to college or anything," she had to say to defend herself at one point. "We just think that we're shortchanging the kids with their education if we don't teach them about finances, budgeting, and work with a small business." Again the word "work." Like most American teenagers, our kids played way too many video games and my wife saw the venture as a potential solution.

In the end, I think her friends were a little less suspicious than mine but still not too supportive. Maybe my buddies felt it was a personal attack on their choice of career to look for something more. Whatever the case, the word was out. The neighborhood would be watching and not just for prowlers.

Maybe my wife felt a little isolated without any support from her friends and my inability to stay engaged in a conversation for more than five minutes about the color coordination of a gift basket or what cheese went with which cracker. Bottom line, she had to reach out to family.

She had always shared a special relationship with her aunt, and this aunt was a perfect fit for discussions about the configuration of gift baskets. (I assumed this because of the amount of decorations and trinkets carefully placed around her home.)

Of course, I was wrong. I quickly realized the purpose of the phone call to her aunt, and the follow-up lunch across town, was not about gift baskets but about getting encouragement.

As my wife had hoped, that's exactly what she got. Her aunt was thrilled with her new venture in life and all that it embodied. Apparently, back in the day she had once owned and operated a gift shop. They talked for hours about her own experiences with the American Dream and entrepreneurship.

I provided the best emotional support I could and gave the thumbs-up to any gift basket that included chocolate, golf balls, or movie tickets. Apparently I was no match for the bonding between my wife and her aunt.

Fortunately, as I expected, my brother was interested and eager to attend Saturday's class when I invited him. I also think he wanted to say "I told you so" about my recent revelation that entrepreneurism could provide much more than I previously thought.

In the end, my wife and I realized that we were going to experience a few changes in our circle of friends because of this new commitment.

Our CPA told us that we would want to build a support structure of friends and/or family to help encourage us. That advice now hit home more than ever.

We were excited about Saturday and weren't giving up.

STRUCTURE

We were joining a new club. The small-business crowd. It was awkward but energizing at the same time.

It was surprising to feel the level of ambition in the air at the seminar. So many people throwing around ideas with pencil and paper in hand, ready to take notes on an idea or the name and number of someone to network with.

It was something I hadn't felt since college. Corporate America doesn't have this feel in its meetings. Too many ulterior motives, politics, and agendas are going on.

There wasn't any fanfare to our CPA's entrance, just a warm welcome and promises of quality education and no-nonsense truths. He started right in with the concept of business ownership and tracking expenses—much of which we had covered in his office. But then the main course was set in front of us, and we couldn't wait to dig in intellectually.

I remember when he announced, "Once you have decided to start your business or even if you have already been operating one for some time . . . how do we structure our business for maximum asset protection, tax savings, and ease of administration?"

It was the question most of us had come to have answered. It was interesting that he spent a good amount of time on administration and how we need to recognize our strengths and weaknesses with organizational skills, bookkeeping, and tolerance for additional checkbooks and paperwork in our lives. He emphasized that having a small business takes at least some attention to detail. "You can't avoid it, just embrace it," he said.

He did, however, give us some hope when he mentioned he would come back to these duties and involving our family members in the business later in the day.

The first point he made about structuring was that it was just as important not to have the wrong business entity as it was to have the correct entity for doing business. He pointed out there were a lot of scams out there and suggested some books on scams and asset protection.

Most importantly, he cautioned us to watch out for non-lawyers setting up companies. In fact, he argued that CPAs shouldn't be providing legal documents and setting up entities for their clients either. The CPA should get on the same page with a client's lawyer to create the right structure, a task more easily said than done.

He also warned us to get a second opinion and to call him if anyone was suggesting entities in Nevada, Delaware, or Wyoming just to save on taxes or hide for some reason. Such a strategy can be helpful in some instances, he said, but realistically, it's for maybe 10 percent of those seeking asset protection or tax savings.

I was expecting him to start explaining the purpose of a corporation, but he took an unexpected turn in the presentation. He started to explain the big picture and business income before he discussed the various types of entities. Again, I was surprised with what he could do with such a difficult and boring topic.

He said, "When we plan for our client's big picture and long-term wealth building, we divide your financial life into two halves: short term and long term. On these two sides we list the type of income or wealth you are building in your business."

The diagram he started with had a line down the middle. Then he started to solicit comments from the group. I started to think of the different types of income. It was a whole new way of looking at things. I liked it and copied the list from the board. (See Figure 3.1.)

It was interesting, some of the distinctions he made in the types of income an entrepreneur might create.

First, he said W-2 income doesn't have a place on either list. It isn't something we can funnel through a business. Moreover, he emphasized tax planning around W-2 income is extremely limited.

Next, he pointed out that short-term income in a business is generally referred to as ordinary income and is subject to self-employment tax. This is a tax of approximately 15.3 percent, and its source is FICA, the tax for Social Security and Medicare. He jokingly called FICA the "f-word."

He mentioned we would discuss how to save on self-employment tax later.

Finally, we discussed the long-term or "passive" income and items such as rent, interest, and capital gains. This topic was especially intriguing because this side of the equation has two major benefits: 1) Taxpayers don't have to pay FICA on passive income, and 2) what

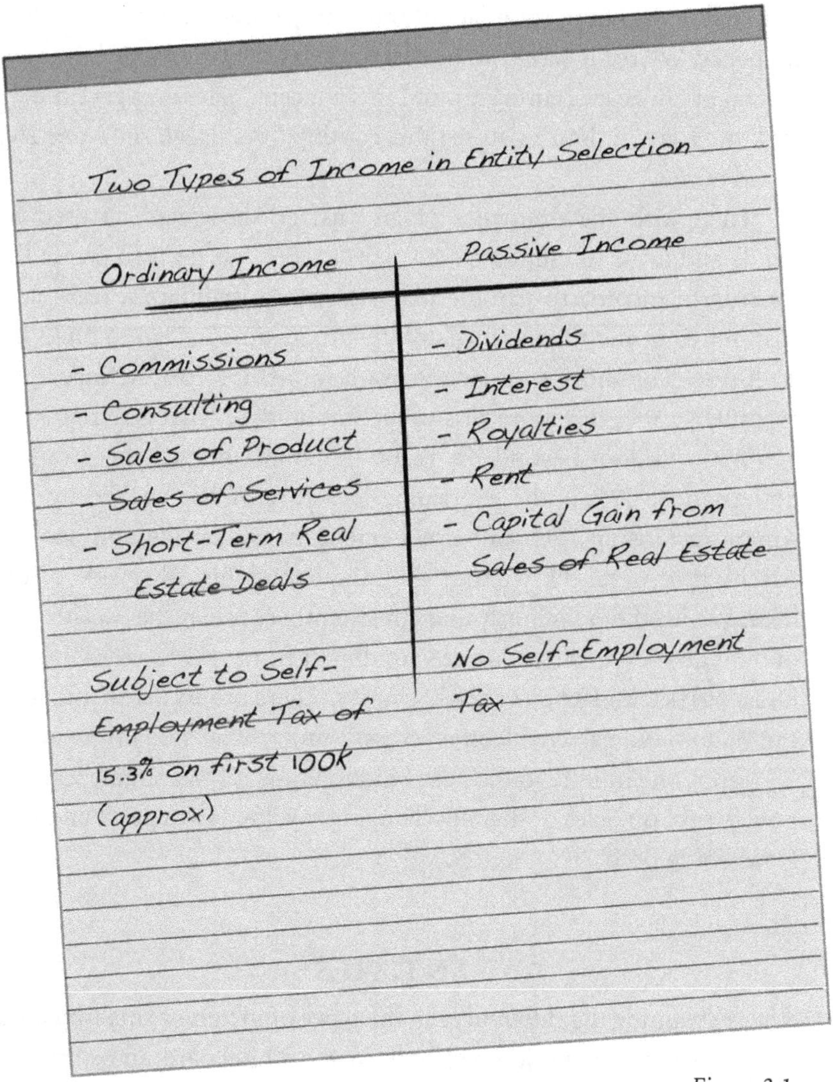

Two Types of Income in Entity Selection

Ordinary Income	Passive Income
- Commissions	- Dividends
- Consulting	- Interest
- Sales of Product	- Royalties
- Sales of Services	- Rent
- Short-Term Real Estate Deals	- Capital Gain from Sales of Real Estate
Subject to Self-Employment Tax of 15.3% on first 100k (approx)	No Self-Employment Tax

Figure 3.1

people are really creating on this side of the equation is net worth and equity.

The passive side is our asset-building side!

My wife looked at me during this discussion with several approving raises of her eyebrows. I whispered to her, "This is the piece we have been talking about in roundabout ways, but couldn't put into words or on paper. We really have two buckets or sides to our financial lives and we can organize everything around this concept." Her eyes gave me the look of "I get it; didn't you see this coming?" As usual, she's one step ahead of me.

Then with the dramatics of an onstage showman, he used his hands and arms to emphasize his words. "See, we need to create this short-term income to pay the bills and try to maintain a reasonable cost of living, and then use whatever extra income we can to build our asset side. The short-term side is just a funnel for creating income to eventually move to a more passive income lifestyle. That is retirement!"

With wisdom beyond his years, he almost begged the group to understand. "This is the overriding structure of our goal to live the American Dream. We can't live a one-dimensional life and just live paycheck to paycheck without thinking about this other side of our lives. We need to religiously and consistently consider the 'wealth' side of our equation and how we are building it from year to year." It's not just a 401(k), an IRA, or Social Security. There are so many things we can do to build passive income and save on taxes all along the way.

From one minute to the next I didn't know if I was simply learning how to save on taxes or literally changing my life. It was deep, and I felt I was doing both.

ENTITIES

After explaining the differences in the types of income a small-business owner may create, he jumped back to the whiteboard and started to quickly sketch one of his soon-to-be-infamous bubble charts.

My brother smiled and rubbed his hands together. This was the type of information seasoned business owners wanted to hear, maybe not so much to learn something new but to confirm they have the right structure themselves and to discuss the new rules for operating and maintaining their entity.

Our CPA started by simply listing the different forms of doing business and drawing a line down the middle. He explained that Sole Proprietorships could be used for short-term or long-term income, while Corporations are for short-term projects and LLCs and LPs are generally for long-term (see Figure 3.2).

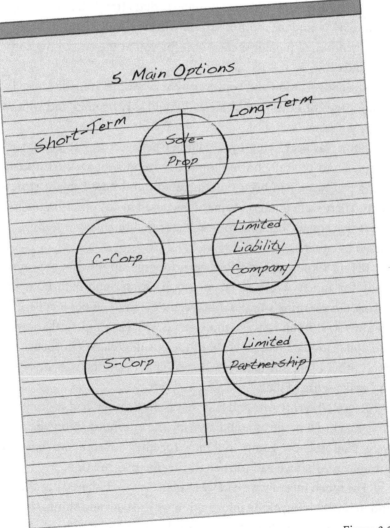

Figure 3.2

Of course, he said there were exceptions to this general rule, and each situation needed to be considered according to its own set of facts and circumstances. However, he took the time to go through every entity, showing the pros and cons, and most importantly, the tax results of using each type of entity.

I took solace in the fact our speaker had created a summary of each entity with diagrams and gave it to those that attended. It was designed in an easy-to-understand format, something I could keep to study and add my notes. (I include a copy of it for you at the end of my story in Appendix B.)

The conversation and concepts were awesome! It made sense. I was taking pages of notes as quickly as I could. My brother and wife were doing the same.

Time was also flying by. I couldn't believe I was enjoying such a complex and typically boring topic. My mind kept racing through all of the projects I had been thinking about and how I might structure them. There were numerous questions posed by the others in the room, and it was equally exciting to hear that my thoughts and feelings were shared by others.

Before I knew it, the CPA began to wrap up his thoughts and get ready for lunch. We had taken a quick water-and-bathroom break during the morning's topics, but I can't ever remember a college class that was so clear and easy to understand with such practical knowledge and applications. I had taken all of the business classes in college, but I don't think I had one teacher who was able to summarize these points and make sense of it all.

Regrettably, my wife and I, as well as my brother, had commitments after lunch. None of us could stay for the afternoon. Nonetheless, we were planning on going to lunch together to compare notes and summarize what we had learned during the presentation.

The lunch meeting we had was a blast. We each shared our thoughts and understanding of the information we learned, and summarized the key points together. Everything seemed to make a lot more sense to me when I bounced the ideas off others.

The two major points my wife gathered centered around the Sole Proprietorship.

First, the Sole Proprietorship was easy and affordable to set up. She really didn't have to file anything with the state or feds unless she wanted to reserve a name, was going to have employees, or needed a business license, which wasn't always necessary for a small-business owner.

Second, she remembered specifically that the three major reasons for a small-business owner to move from a Sole Proprietorship and set up an entity was for asset protection, more advanced tax planning, or for marketing reasons. She was anxious to get started with her business and was glad to hear that setting up a formal entity wasn't absolutely critical.

My brother loved the S-Corporation and the S-Corp power it had for him in his chiropractic practice. We came to realize the S-Corp was the perfect entity for small-business owners creating short-term or "ordinary" income and giving them the ability to save on self-employment tax.

Historically, the Social Security Administration and IRS have hated this strategy, but at the same time, too many taxpayers overpay Social Security and Medicare with minimal or potentially no benefit in the future.

Congress has apparently taken up the issue of the S-Corp and the savings it provides from FICA taxes, but the CPA said that this is still a valid consideration and there are opportunities to save with careful planning.

Timing was also an issue many taxpayers overlooked. Many of us think that when we meet with our CPA in March or April, he or she can wave a magic wand and implement tax strategies for the prior year, perhaps even set up an entity retroactively. The CPA was clear that planning starts NOW and that he can't go back in time to set up a company if we need the savings.

My brother made an appointment with him before we left for lunch.

I was intrigued with the discussion around the C-Corporation. The CPA was adamant that for the overwhelming majority of small-business owners, a C-Corp was completely unnecessary and more costly than it was worth. He also felt it was oversold all over the country, part of the Nevada, Wyoming, and Delaware sales pitch.

Arguably, it was a little too much to digest for some with the diagrams and numbers he was throwing on the board. He gave us a handout comparing the S-Corp and C-Corp, and I have included that at the end of this story (see Appendix C).

Personally, I was intrigued with the discussion about Limited Liability Companies (LLCs), and all of us were surprised to understand their basic purpose. Essentially, LLCs don't save taxes. They are formed for two major reasons: asset protection and partnering.

Apparently, Limited Partnerships (LPs) were taxed very similar to LLCs, but were used in unique ways for asset protection, estate planning, and gifting for tax purposes.

The CPA didn't pontificate too much on the asset protection issues with LLCs and LPs and how they protect assets OR protect the owners from the operations. Regarding the partnership issue, he said CPAs loved the LLC and so did lawyers to document partnerships and split income and expenses between partners. However, they are generally not built for tax planning or minimizing self-employment tax and need to be used carefully. The beauty is that any person or entity can own an LLC. Thus, you could have your S-Corp own an LLC or even your revocable living trust.

I included several informational pieces the CPA gave us that will give you additional guidance on the pros and cons of all this entity stuff in Appendix B.

Bottom line, we were amazed not so much how simple the topic was but at how this CPA organized it so we could get our heads around it and organize the issues.

We felt empowered and ready for the next step in our quest to achieve the American Dream!

SUMMARY
Foundations

I am absolutely serious when I say that having the right support structure in your social and family life is just as important as setting up the right type of legal structure for your business.

Friends and Family

Let your family know about your inner desire to build a small business and the sacrifices you are willing to make. Tell them about your dreams, your excitement, and the positive impact it will have on you and those around you. If these individuals aren't supportive, avoid them or at least the topic when you are with them.

Networking is a must. Start getting acquainted with other business owners. Join some networking groups, the local chamber, investment clubs, whatever it takes to start tapping into good supportive friends and associates.

Choice of Entity

Remember, you don't have to have an entity to start a small business. Sometimes beginning as a Sole Proprietorship is the best structure to utilize. However, when there is liability exposure, a need for a marketing image, or the threat of higher taxes looming over you, it's time to set up a formal entity.

The odds-on favorite for the small-business owner producing ordinary income is the S-Corp. It allows for savings on self-employment tax and gives liability protection.

For holding rental property, the LLC is absolutely the best entity to use, and if you are trying to protect some high-value investments, an LP might be an important consideration.

Bottom line, a CPA should not be setting up your entity and should be working with you and your attorney to make a plan.

See Appendix B and C at the end of this book for more detailed explanations and diagrams of each entity.

CONCEPT

4

TECHNIQUES IN
BUSINESS PLANNING

PLANNING TO FAIL

My wife was gung-ho to start her gift basket company, and yet she was trying to follow our CPA's advice of taking baby steps and not moving too quickly.

She had also really embraced the family support concept and had started spending more and more time with her aunt, who was eager to share all of the juicy details of the business and her experiences owning a gift shop years earlier.

Little did I know it was much more than that. In female terms they were bonding as well as imparting advice to one another.

Like any wise husband, I was careful not to ask too many questions. They actually may have started to talk with me about all of the heartache and tears, while of course glossing over the business aspects of the saga.

What I did glean from my wife, or I should say she was determined to inform me about, was the actual history regarding her aunt's business. I didn't know it, but her aunt had gone through a divorce and then a remarriage during the time she owned the business.

Her aunt was convinced, and probably rightfully so, that the business destroyed her first marriage. She shared experience after experience of not making wise decisions regarding the startup of the business and its operations. She hired the wrong employees, signed a bad lease, worked with the wrong vendors. The stories went on and on. Apparently she went through the school of hard knocks and got her full money's worth.

Come to find out, she and her first husband didn't look for any outside support through the process, something that was a constant and contentious issue between them. He was a do-it-yourself kind of guy and was convinced they could figure things out themselves, undoubtedly only contributing to a lot of their mistakes.

Planning was not an option and rarely implemented. Lawyers, CPAs, and advisors were considered too expensive. They constantly stepped over the dollar to pick up a nickel, and her aunt felt that every dime they saved on getting advice or taking time for education cost them $10 in lost opportunity, revenue, or mistakes. Her husband didn't see it this way.

In the end, the marriage failed, and in the divorce he gave her the entire business—assets and debts. He blamed the business for their breakup. My wife's aunt felt there was a lot more to it, which there probably was.

Bottom line, her aunt ended up learning a lot of principles the hard way.

I thought this tale of disappointment was going to discourage my wife from a business startup completely, but then she immediately dove into Act II of the story.

After the divorce her aunt focused on the training and support she always wanted from some affordable outside sources, and the business began to flourish. Her entire self-image and self-esteem changed and improved, and of course that is when Mr. Right came along.

It was the makings of a made-for-TV movie on Lifetime (a channel I avoid like the plague), but for my wife and her aunt, the result was a storybook ending.

The two proprietors fell in love with each other and with the business. They ultimately opened two more locations and then sold the business a few years ago for a significant profit.

This was all news to me, yet I had always wondered where their retirement had come from and noticed Social Security wasn't paying for their lifestyle.

In the end, I have to be honest and admit that seeing their healthy retirement income and hearing about their small-business venture actually invigorated me as well. The story was tragic in the beginning but had a wonderful ending.

I almost shed a tear. Well, maybe it wasn't the story that made me so emotional. I actually looked at my 401(k) balance that same evening and thought of the equity they had built up and then sold in the business compared to the incredible matching by my employer to my retirement plan—NOT!

The eerie part of the story was the proof of the age-old adage: If you fail to plan, then plan to fail.

Apparently, my wife's aunt had said time and time again that there was a significant lack of planning in the business with her first husband, but there was a complete change of perspective toward planning after the divorce.

In the last seminar with the CPA, he emphasized that it was not uncommon for business owners to decide on a new business idea but then struggle on the next steps to take. Setting up the right entity was just a very small part of the process.

What about a business plan, marketing, defining the product or service, deciding on the right piece of real estate, and then financing? Just to name a few.

In addition to the baby steps concept, we were grateful that the CPA brought up the words "Strategic Planning" in his seminar. We weren't able to stick around for that piece of the presentation, but it was certainly on our radar at that point.

As luck would have it, this Strategic Planning concept was something my wife's aunt was completely behind and was glad to hear that we had already been receiving some education and consulting.

And although we had missed the live seminar on the planning topic, we were excited to hear that the CPA had recorded a host of webinar/videos on his website on this topic as well as others.

My wife and her aunt were planning on watching videos every night this week after some chick flicks on Lifetime. I was anxious to get the report on what they learned . . . from the CPA videos, not *Pride and Prejudice.*

THREE DIFFERENT PLANS

While my wife and her aunt were diving headfirst into the gift basket business, I was still more interested in that little rental property I had come across. I wanted to take some active steps to purchase it, but was unsure of myself. It seemed the more I learned, the more I realized I didn't know. Isn't life peculiar that way? Interestingly enough, it's education that tends to be the best antidote.

My wife had encouraged me to sit down and watch some more videos and webinars, but I didn't think they would really apply to real estate. I would soon discover I was wrong. Nevertheless, she didn't give up. She kept watching, and she shared with me every little thing she learned.

It was actually refreshing in our marriage to have some different topics to discuss and to share a common interest in something new.

The part that fascinated me the most was what she was learning about small-business planning. She was very clear in telling me, "A Business Plan is very different from your Marketing Plan and Strategic Plan. Each one serves a different purpose in the startup and operation of your business."

I asked, "You wouldn't have a diagram of this by chance, would you?" She smiled and said, "I thought you might say that." (See Figure 4.1.)

She explained that her Business Plan was the "write-up" to see if the numbers made sense, who her competition was, and what her product mix may be, just to name a few items.

With her characteristic excitement she said, "My business plan helped me figure out the pricing for my different gift baskets and my target market, and forced me to lay out my vendors and confirm my production costs."

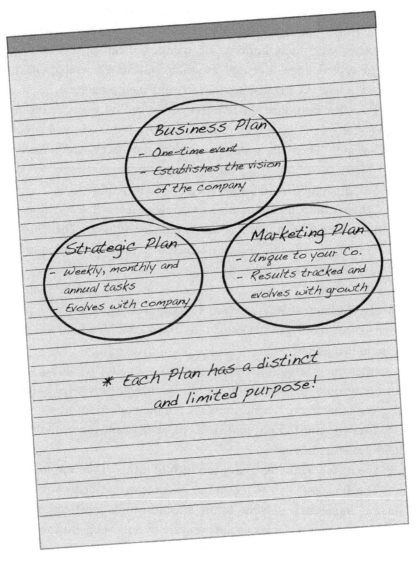

Figure 4.1

She showed me her plan. I was pretty impressed with the whole document. If she polished it up a little, our CPA said she could take it to the bank and apply for a small-business loan through the SBA or some other program.

He also indicated there were a host of ways to raise money for a small business, and new business owners should take time to familiarize themselves with these options. He mentioned borrowing, investors, venture capital, angel investors, as well as state and federal grants, just to name a few. We made notes to start studying up on these.

The CPA cautioned us, however, to be careful with the business credit scam that has proliferated across America. My wife quoted him, saying, "There are certainly ways you can secure credit lines for your business without going through a traditional SBA loan, but your personal guarantee is almost always going to be required.

"These companies out there offering unsecured credit lines are deceiving lenders through one application or another. They also use the term 'shelf corporation' as the vehicle to get you there. Bottom line, they are scams to avoid like the plague."

We felt our CPA was a savvy businessman and had been around the block. I know that if there was a way to do it legitimately, he would have figured it out and suggested it to us. So I felt his advice was pretty close to being right on.

After our rousing discussion on the options for obtaining capital for our business and the scams out there, my wife proceeded to tell me she was going to put her Business Plan in the drawer, for now anyway.

"Are you nuts?" I responded. "Look at all of the time you put into it." I was incredulous.

She merely said, "You have so much to learn." Then she smiled.

The Business Plan is the initial document that helps you decide on the framework of your future business and, most importantly, determine if it is a viable business venture or not. Many Business Plans reveal that you should not start a particular business. But once you are finished with a Business Plan you can potentially use to obtain financing, you pull out two more critical pieces before it goes into the drawer: the Strategic Plan and Marketing Plan.

These two dynamic plans become your best friends and should be used almost on a daily basis to implement your Business Plan. They should be broken down into daily, monthly, and annual tasks to make your business a success.

I sat back, and after thinking for a moment I felt that really made a lot of sense. It went back to our CPA's comment about "not trying to bite off more than you can chew."

As the week pressed on, my wife was sharing more and more concepts with me regarding her plans and the insights her aunt was giving her as well. However, every time she wanted to dive into the details of the daily plans she was implementing, I forced her to go back and talk about her Business Plan.

Obviously, as a corporate executive, I knew my company had all sorts of "planning" documents created on a regular basis. Do we tackle this product, or expand into that market, or align ourselves with a partner or a particular vendor? It was a common procedure, so I didn't feel that intimidated by the topic.

Nevertheless, I had a healthy level of interest regarding what was needed for a small-business Business Plan. I didn't know what sections were most critical for the bank or even me as I determined whether the project was viable.

My wife said it was a little much to try to teach it to me. She felt she was learning it all too quickly herself. However, she gave me another great summary document created by our CPA. I included it for you at the end of this story as well. (See Appendix D.)

Again, I thought to myself, "Where would I find this information if my CPA didn't have it to give to me?" I suppose Google would have done the trick, but internet searches can only do so much. I was grateful for the resource.

As soon as I was up to speed on the business plan concept, my wife said she would give me my daily "battle plan." I didn't know what this was, but was afraid it was just another creative word for a honey-do list. Little did I know it would be another tool that would change my life.

BATTLE PLANS

As we discussed it, apparently my wife had been designing her implementation plans with tasks or checklists that she needed to complete over the next three months and that was helping her feel like it was manageable.

She was "waiting" to get started selling, but had plenty to do in order to get to that point. She had actually started to produce some baskets and had some demos floating around. She was also starting to build some strategic partnerships, something my wife said was a critical part of her perfect Marketing Plan.

"I know sales will increase over time as I work out the kinks, test my product, get to know my customers, and not try to rush into it too quickly," she said confidently.

The CPA had been prepping her though his online education resources and phone calls to "stay the course" and be "optimistically cautious." He had taught her that there were a number of reasons why small businesses fail in the first year or two, and some of them are out of the business owner's control. But most are not.

This is where the Strategic Plan came into the picture.

Essentially, this was a document broken down into monthly, quarterly, and annual tasks. Sometimes there were weekly tasks and sometimes more long-term tasks that were out two to three years. But in the end it needed to be manageable and realistic.

To me, there were two fascinating aspects to this whole procedure. The first was the concept of a "Daily Battle Plan." This stemmed from the situation many of us face every day!

We have those moments on the drive home from work or while lying in bed at night when we realize what those critical tasks are that we need to complete the next day. You know the ones: call so-and-so, get that e-mail off, send that form via overnight mail, and so on.

But what happens? We sit down at our office chair first thing in the morning and get attacked by all of the problems demanding our immediate attention. We get hammered with e-mails, phone calls, and unscheduled meetings. All of a sudden it's noon.

The result: The most critical items of the day don't get completed. And if we are trying to implement a weekly or monthly strategic plan, we immediately get off course. All of a sudden we aren't reaching our goals and meeting our personally imposed deadlines. We get frustrated and take it out on ourselves. Our self-esteem as a business owner suffers, and we can easily go into a downward spiral with our business concept.

The Daily Battle Plan was the solution. At the end of the day, before you go to bed, or first thing in the morning, you take out a sticky note and write down the three to five things that you HAVE to have finished that day, items critical to your short- and long-term plans.

Then before you do anything else, you finish those items. It's amazing how empowering and life changing this simple procedure can be.

Now, are there emergencies and critical interruptions from time to time? Absolutely. But if we stay focused on this system, amazingly our Strategic Plan starts to move forward and our business progresses.

I realize there have been countless books written on this universal problem for business owners, managers, and anyone with a life! However, this little system helped me and my wife tremendously.

The second surprising aspect of the Strategic Plan was the admonition from our CPA to carry it around with us EVERYWHERE we went. Carry it on the airplane and trips; keep it by the computer and your nightstand. Basically, have it near you at all times so you can add notes to it when you're inspired with ideas and tasks to enhance the plans for your business.

And use it! Check off items you complete. Of course, my favorite little strategy is putting items on it I have already done and then checking them off. It always makes me feel a little more productive.

Whenever I asked my wife about her plans, she immediately pulled out her Strategic Plan to show me the timeline of her business model. It was pretty cool.

The shock to me the last time she pulled it out was that it really wasn't a big to-do list, it actually had categories, benchmarks, and timelines.

This is where things got a little more complicated to explain, but she showed me a basic design the CPA had given her. I loved it! It was broken into critical sections for the management of the business, and numerical goals were included whenever possible.

For example, my wife said, "I have a triggering factor that once we are producing x number of gift baskets per week, then I am allowed to purchase an additional workbench and storage shelves for product." She had figured out her assembly line needs and the space and equipment needed to produce a certain number of baskets per week. I had to admit I was impressed.

To help you out, I've included a typical Strategic Plan at the end of this story that can serve as a template for you to design your own plan. (See Appendix E.)

I then started to press my wife about her sales goals and how she was going to pull it off. That is when she brought up her "perfect" Marketing Plan. I asked her what was so perfect about it. I was pleasantly surprised with the answer.

THE PERFECT MARKETING PLAN

My wife was so excited when she told me that she had really only implemented about 10 percent of her Marketing Plan, but that she wasn't ready to kick it into full gear either. She was trying to grow with baby steps and work out as many kinks as she could.

I asked her what was so perfect about her particular plan and what it looked like. It was interesting to see that it was broken down into all sorts of cool categories. Areas such as print material, branding for her logo, website, social networking, direct mail, and strategic partnerships.

However, according to our CPA, that's not what made it perfect. Rather, it was the fact that the plan was tailored to her business. Not every business can have the same Marketing Plan. And although that seems obvious, a lot of business owners make the mistake of following the same steps as everyone else to market their business.

Specifically, our CPA said many small-business owners have to learn the hard way that marketing is different from advertising. Marketing is much more than just placing some ads somewhere. Marketing is choosing a distinct set of strategies that will directly impact and create sales in a business.

We learned, for example, that some businesses are finding a lot of success with the social networking boom and using Twitter, Facebook, and YouTube to attract new customers. Others are realizing that staying with bread-and-butter networking and one-on-one referral sources is the most powerful strategy.

Moreover, it's important to identify early on whether or not print advertising such as brochures, signage, and newspaper ads is really going to have an impact for your business.

Every business is different!

The more I looked at it, the more I realized my wife was just scratching the surface of her Marketing Plan.

In fact, I was surprised at all of the ideas for marketing she had actually come up with and complimented her on her creativity. Come to find out, however, she had implemented a Board of Advisors concept that our CPA gave her when talking about a foundation of friends and family as support.

Again, her aunt was a huge support to her in this area. It wasn't so much that her aunt had all the answers and creative marketing strategies up her sleeve specific to gift baskets. It was just nice for my wife to have a sounding board for ideas and some moral support along the way.

Now, I have to admit that when I think of a Board of Advisors, I think of a room with a big mahogany conference table and old, tough faces looking at me giving me advice as I hold my tail between my legs.

My wife's board consisted of her best friends and aunt going to lunch twice a week to talk about the business and get her friends' ideas. Of course, lunch was on my wife, but she said it was some of the best money spent on the business. She was getting amazing ideas from her friends, and ironically everyone loved to share their knowledge.

It's interesting that most of us love to give advice and share our thoughts in exchange for a little food and a kind thank you. Her little power lunches with her Board of Advisors was already paying big dividends.

And although I thought the myriad ideas listed in her plan were pretty neat, probably the most insightful aspect of the Marketing Plan was that under each category there were four criteria that had to be explained and identified. They were the purpose, procedure, statistical goal, and budget for each particular strategy.

Her aunt felt this was ingenious and wished her own Marketing Plan had been so well organized years ago. She admitted that in essence she followed the same procedure, but not as well designed and planned as my wife was doing.

For example, in her own gift shop her aunt had made it a goal to ask all customers where they had heard of the shop and why they came in. Then under the counter she kept a little tally of the responses and tried to identify her best marketing strategies with this numerical data.

Our CPA said that we could not underestimate the power of the numbers. This may, of course, seem an obvious admonition from a CPA, but these weren't numbers on a tax return. These were actual numbers showing referral sources and where the dollars were coming from.

My wife was already setting some goals with different strategies, but was strongly cautioned by her Board of Advisors not to get too attached to any one marketing concept. Her aunt said it was shocking for her to find out what strategies actually worked, and over time she was better able to focus and channel her marketing dollars.

Again, I was grateful to see that the CPA had given her a basic Marketing Plan model, which my wife was carrying around with her everywhere she went so she could make additions and revisions anytime. But the basic structure was always there with all its potential categories and options to consider. I have included more details on building a Marketing Plan at the end of my story. (See Appendix F.)

Now just a few months after our initial seminar with the CPA, I was pretty excited for my wife and how her project was developing.

However, in my little world I was still looking for a good rental property and was frustrated that I wasn't making as much progress as she was. I had built a Strategic Plan, but I was floundering and a little jealous my wife was making more headway than I.

Of course, as we all know, these sorts of things show their ugly heads in relationships, and one particular evening a fairly heated discussion arose because of my frustration. Basically, I was upset, and I took it out on her. She knew it and was understanding.

She again showed me some of her newfound wisdom and said, "Don't worry . . . in time the property that you are supposed to buy will present itself. Just keep looking and learning."

As I was walking away downtrodden, anxious to see what was on Sports Center that night, she stuck her head around the corner and said, "You know, our CPA is speaking at some real estate course this next week. You ought to check it out."

It hit me like a ton a bricks. I needed more education on this real estate thing to take away my fear and stop the procrastination. I also thought of my brother as a key part of my future Board of Advisors, and maybe he would be able to go with me.

I would have to call in sick for a couple days next week. Of course, not with the flu, just sick of working there.

SUMMARY
Techniques in Business Planning

When starting a small business, we all know it takes a lot more than a good idea to succeed. Even wise tax and legal planning won't guarantee success or prevent failure. Ongoing Business Planning is the key to our ultimate success and needs to be taken seriously.

If you are contemplating a new project, creating a *Business Plan* is the first step in the right direction whether or not you plan on seeking capital. It can give you the road map to get your business off the ground, instill confidence in your investor(s), and at the very least tell you if your idea is a good or a bad one.

Once you open your doors, the Business Plan is rarely used, even though many people hate to admit it. However, there are two other plans that are a by-product of the process: a dynamic Strategic Plan and Marketing Plan.

The *Strategic Plan* should be reviewed monthly at the least. It lays out the specific things you should do in your business over the next three months to three years. It will be constantly changing and evolving as your business grows. Carry it around with you everywhere you go, and follow it.

Your *Marketing Plan* is the companion to your Strategic Plan and just as valuable to your business. This plan should encompass every method you are utilizing to bring in sales. Question every one of your new customers to determine which strategies are making the phone ring or causing people to walk through the door.

Finally, use a ***Board of Advisors*** to help hold you accountable to your plans and force you to look at the big picture. These family, friends, or professional advisors can give you advice and emotional support. Meet with them regularly.

See the Appendices at the end of this book for more detailed explanations of a Business Plan, Strategic Plan, and Marketing Plan.

CONCEPT

5

RENTAL
REAL ESTATE

THE VEIL LIFTED

Maybe I had been watching too many Wall Street-sponsored shows on CNN or Fox the last few years, but I was really jaded about real estate. I thought it was a "'bottom-feeder" approach to building wealth.

Isn't that how it is portrayed in mainstream financial planning media? Because of this propaganda, my buddies at work and I had truly believed that there were only two types of individuals that really invested in real estate.

The first type was the one we would mock at work whenever possible. They worked in the trenches of real estate every day, and had given up on a college degree or a real job years ago.

We would arbitrarily classify most professions in real estate as contractors, realtors, and self-professed real estate investors that read every book and listened to every CD produced on the topic.

We had simply convinced ourselves that they weren't as educated as we were or they wouldn't be doing real estate. We had real jobs or so we thought.

The second type were the ones we envied but believed we could never emulate. They were the rich who bought real estate because they had super amounts of cash and credit to do it, that is, the Donald Trumps and megadevelopers in every city around the country.

Deep down, we believed real estate investment to be a legitimate way to build wealth, but only IF we had enough cash to do it right. If not, we would have to fight it out with the bottom-feeders, the real estate professionals, and take the verbal abuse of the financial magazine experts.

However, since my "transformation" as I was now calling it, I had discovered that more and more people owned little rental properties on the side but had kept it a secret for some reason or other. People I never even imagined would own real estate were turning out to be "closet real estate investors."

When I opened my mind a little, I also discovered that most of the wealth built in the United States has been made in real estate and that the average returns on real estate had outperformed the S&P 500 over the past 50 years. These were little-known facts that the Wall Street money machine didn't want us average Americans to know.

Of course, it didn't surprise me that when I told my brother I was going to check out a seminar on real estate in a week or two, he was very interested in coming to the classes with me. As before, it was more comforting to have a partner in crime when heading to these types of seminars rather than go by myself.

I was still trying to shed my corporate mentality and prejudices toward this fringe group of real estate investors, the very people I had maligned in the past. I was repenting.

The real estate seminar the CPA was speaking at had a broader curriculum of classes than I expected. It was actually exciting and refreshing to see it really wasn't a one-size-fits-all class scenario.

When I called my CPA to get his advice on going to the training and what classes to take, he lined me up for several courses on types of real estate investing and then made me promise to take his class on taxes.

I agreed, and in turn he promised me his tax strategies on real estate would bring the whole thing together and I would love it! I believed him as usual. He hadn't let me down yet.

The much-anticipated day of the training courses arrived. My brother and I were pumped and came with pencil and pad in hand ready to go. The first two classes were indeed a whirlwind. It was like a crash course on corporate politics, mergers, and acquisitions—but only for real estate.

I was actually pleased to discover that most of my business and corporate training was actually paying off. I could crunch numbers much faster than the novice investors, and I could foresee risks and rewards a little more quickly from my experience with projects in the corporate world.

Nonetheless, I still learned a ton. It forced me to nail down my vision of real estate investing and what was the best plan for me. I learned the basics about analyzing good rental properties vs. good fix-and-flips. I also realized there was still a little truth to the late-night TV "no money down" concept.

I had always dismissed those late-night infomercials as plastic magic scams for the unsuspecting, simply there to entice me to part with my credit card number on a whim. I really never believed that someone could buy real estate with little or no money down. I was wrong.

Come to find out that with the downturn in the real estate market, owner financing, subject-to financing, partnering with other investors, and bank-owned properties were much more prevalent than I realized.

In fact, I was taught that in any real estate market, one could always find a deal. One just had to be diligent and patient.

In the first three days of the training, it seemed as if I had discovered another financial market or trading floor akin to Wall Street or the NASDAQ. The beauty was that the trading floor was all around me. It was like a veil had been lifted from my eyes, and I could see this whole new world that had previously been hidden to me.

Damn corporate America and its control of mainstream news and media! They had truly demonized the real estate investor and its lure.

My brother probably soaked in a little more than I because he didn't have to overcome all of the preconceived notions and prejudices I was having to battle. He was drawn immediately to the fix-and-flip strategy, as savvy investors had coined it. It was pretty straightforward—buy low, fix it up, sell high.

However, because that proposition is easier said than done, we learned that we had to be careful and plan for the fall-back strategy; that if we couldn't sell a project, it should always end up being a quality rental property.

Good real estate investors always had a fall-back strategy and never bought simply for appreciation. I think more people wish they had learned and lived that principle before the real estate crash of 2008.

My brother pulled me aside in the hall at one point during a break and pummeled me with a bunch of ideas. One of his more persuasive arguments was that we could go in together on a fix-and-flip and share in the investment. One of us could do the work, and the other could throw in the cash.

Of course I immediately asked, "Who puts in the cash, and who puts in the work?" He just kept rambling on with his harebrained scheme until I said more forcefully, "Hold on . . . who puts in the cash and who puts in the work?" He just stared at me.

Smirking, I then said, "You mean I put in the cash, and you put in the work."

He immediately agreed, put his hand out to shake hands, and announced, "Well, that is mighty nice of you, bro. I think that is a great idea. Let's do it."

I, of course, realized this is what brothers were good for, but actually I wasn't complaining. I was slammed at work, and it could maybe just work.

He put his arm around me as we walked down the hall and reminded me, "Dude, we could really work this if we're careful. Worst-case scenario, we end up with a couple rental properties this year that break even on the holding costs, and we split the risk in the process."

I actually believed him and was immediately nervous and sick to my stomach. I don't know if it was because I was nervous for the project and the potential of a brighter future, or my brother personally alienating me from all future family reunions with the lawsuit to come.

Oh, well, I was feeling good about it in concept, and we were certainly going to have to put some ideas on paper to make sure we were on the same page. It was business planning time!

The courses over several days were exciting and set the stage each night for a lot of brainstorming at Dennys over numerous Grand Slam specials.

However, I was still actually looking forward to the energy and enthusiasm of my CPA's presentation the next day. I was intrigued as to how this worked into my master tax plan, as he had termed it.

Again, I would have to have faith that my CPA could bring all of this together and make sense of it, something I used to think was impossible for any CPA.

HIDDEN WISDOM

My brother wasn't as thrilled about the tax piece of the training that week. However, I was starting to think taxes made the world go round, at least in America, and the main reason for my relationship with this CPA was to learn new tax strategies.

I knew that I was becoming sick and twisted with this new approach to finance, but I loved saving money on the number-one cost in my life—taxes.

Interestingly enough, I was discovering that it was easier to save on taxes than I realized . . . I just needed to be patient.

The CPA reinforced this point when he started his tax class at the seminar by saying, "This is not a get-rich-quick scheme. I have a master plan to create long-term tax savings beyond your wildest dreams, but it isn't going to happen overnight."

I felt like I was listening to Mr. Wonka at the chocolate factory. It was exciting. Of course, I was thinking of Gene Wilder. The new Wonka, that is, Johnny Depp, freaked me out. I assumed he did the same to most kids, too.

As usual, the CPA started with a diagram that set forth the framework for our discussion. He was confident that there were four benefits to rental real estate and that we needed to look at the big picture to see the overall impact. I took quick notes as usual. (See Figure 5.1.)

After he got the diagram up, I was a little concerned when he said rental real estate. I thought he was going to bring up the benefits of real estate as a whole. I rarely raised my hand in classes, but I had to ask what I was missing and why the focus on only rentals to begin with.

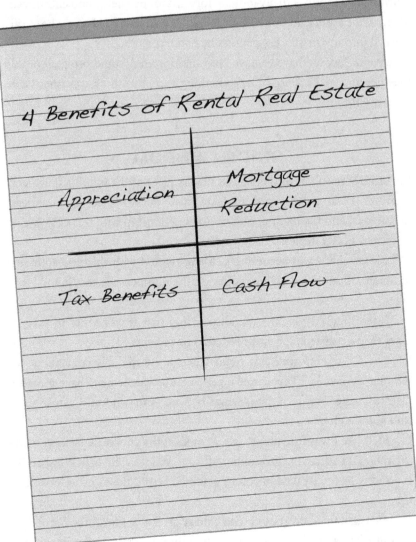

Figure 5.1

He took me back to our first meeting when we talked about short-term and long-term income. "Remember, our ultimate goal is to build our assets on the right side of the equation and create more passive income," he explained. "If you want to do short-term real estate deals, awesome! Get a strategy that works for you, and use your S-Corp for protection as well as to save on the self-employment (SE) tax if you have a certain level of income."

Continuing with his point, he emphasized, "Whether or not you do short-term real estate deals and no matter what your occupation is, I recommend that every one of my clients buy at least one rental property a year!"

I found myself distracted for a moment, thinking that his comment was a fairly bold statement. He realized this and immediately encouraged all of us to be patient and hear how the reasoning played out.

He then made a foundational point that I won't forget: "Remember, we don't want to buy a cruddy rental property, just for the sake of our goal of buying a property every year. We need to make sure we have the capital or a creative acquisition strategy to make it happen properly; we want to buy quality rental property. Absolutely no speculation on appreciation as the principal return on investment is allowed. That is cream on the top over time."

Again his comment was eerie as I thought back to one of my brother's nightmare rental properties he had told us about countless times. I looked at him out of the corner of my eye. As I leaned over to say something condescending, he beat me to it, "Don't say it. At least I have two good rentals." And he smiled.

He was right. At least he had two quality rentals. To him I was still a virgin investor, as he liked to term it. Another quality of a good family member is that he will demean you whenever possible. Two could play at that game, however. I liked to point out that although I was a little late to the party, I didn't have the baggage either. We both knew what the other was thinking and smiled about it.

The CPA caught my attention again when he started pointing to the first benefit with his index finger and focusing the group on his presentation. "The first benefit is of course appreciation. It's tax free and over the long run fairly predictable," he pointed out. "It consistently outperforms the stock market, but we have to be patient with the ups and downs."

I nodded in agreement. He reminded us again that we don't buy property solely for this purpose but can take solace in the fact that if we buy wisely, we can't lose the dirt.

Most people stuck in rental property from the real estate meltdown will admit they bought property they shouldn't have. They purchased in the market craze, hoping for the upswing in value that they assumed would never end.

"Bottom line," he said, "appreciation is tax free until we sell, and there are all sorts of tax strategies to use when we ultimately do sell. For example, 1031 exchanges, installment sales, and charitable remainder trusts just to name a few. These strategies may minimize tax, defer tax into the future, or avoid it altogether." These were topics he said we would discuss at another time, or we could check out his video classroom on his website.

The second benefit he pointed out was mortgage reduction. Simply stated, if our property is breaking even, typically defined as the rent payment covering the mortgage payment, property taxes, and insurance, we were building tax-deferred or even tax-free equity.

Otherwise stated, if our mortgage payment is being paid by the rent, we aren't coming out of pocket, and the mortgage balance is going down in a self-sustaining manner. The equity is growing without being directly related to appreciation and without additional investment by us.

I loved it, and he was making sense!

"Number three," he announced, "is the sexy part! The best of the four benefits. Tax savings, for two big reasons. First, there's depreciation and mortgage interest. The renter is paying the mortgage for us, and we get the write-off for the interest. Combine that with the depreciation deduction offered by the IRS, and oftentimes a property will be losing money on paper."

Now I was confused.

"I thought you wanted your property making money, not losing money," I blurted out as I raised my hand. I immediately was a little self-conscious for popping off a quick question. I normally just don't yell out in a presentation like that, but I was into it and couldn't hold back.

He loved the return enthusiasm and replied, "Remember, you're losing money on paper." He emphasized the words "on paper." "You may be cash flowing, but that is not what is on the tax return."

Continuing, as he was truly on a roll, "Before explaining depreciation and what I mean by paper loss, let me set forth the second reason why there is a huge tax benefit to rental real estate."

He reminded me of the above-the-line concept from our first meeting. He said that we would be moving as many previously personal expenses as possible to the now legitimate expenses needed to manage rental property.

He used travel expenses as an important example. He grinned from ear to ear as he said, "I want you buying your rentals where you are going to be traveling on a regular basis. I need you trying to combine business reasons for your travel with personal trips. Buy a rental near your kids in college and have them manage it. Buy a rental near your in-laws where you travel for the holidays."

He went on with incredible ideas for legitimately splitting up expenses for travel, home office, dining, and between business and personal. Again, he reminded us that we also had to be careful and not be too greedy. "Pigs get fat, and hogs get slaughtered! I don't want you cooking the books with erroneous deductions. Nevertheless, I'm sure all of us can think of thousands of dollars of expenditures that could be legitimately related to our rental properties."

I was mesmerized, and the confusion was gone. "Damn, he's good!" I said to my brother. "Does your CPA open your eyes to planning like that?" He just said, "Shut up, Richard." Another Tommy Boy throwback quote. He was always an SNL fan and followed its actors religiously.

The CPA then brought the whole principle together by explaining the deductions for deprecation and interest, and the entire host of deductions on paper we would use to cause the rental to lose money, even though we had a renter paying the mortgage and were getting long-term appreciation to boot.

"Finally, don't forget number four," he bellowed from the stage, with four fingers held up, "Cash flow!"

My brother nodded to me and smiled. He had actually experienced this with his two good properties.

You can actually have losses on paper, but still have cash flow when rent exceeds your holding costs. "Think about it," the CPA said as he ran some numbers on the board. "You could have rent exceed your mortgage payment by $200 to $300 a month, but by the time you write off depreciation, you have a loss! And we're just getting started."

He told us stories of clients that were making thousands of dollars in cash flow a month and paying zero in taxes. Could it be true? I hate it when things sound too good to be true. I needed more confirmation on this.

Then as if he could read my mind, he sensed the concerns of many in the room.

"I know many of you have had your CPA tell you that you make too much money to write off the losses from your real estate. However, that is a very serious overgeneralization many CPAs make on behalf of their clients. This is because they don't want to take the time to plan and educate their clients on the possibilities of real estate."

And then much to my surprise, he said, "After lunch I'll discuss the good, the bad, and the ugly about those real estate losses. You'll get to write them off, the question is just when and how." I was surprised when I looked down at my watch. I couldn't believe that a couple of hours had flown by so quickly.

He had covered a few of the basics about short-term and long-term income. Something we learned in our first meeting, but it was a great review. But then to learn about these benefits of real estate and how it brought all of the concepts we had learned that week together was absolutely astonishing.

I was really looking forward to lunch. My wife was bringing the kids downtown with her aunt to grab a bite to eat with us. I couldn't wait to tell her what we were learning. I was just hoping she wouldn't be so jealous that I would have to give her my ticket for the class and take the kids to the mall or something.

As my brother and I were trying to summarize the morning's topics and take bites of food between our excited but disjointed explanations, the completely unexpected happened. My kids started asking more questions than my wife, and a whole new world opened up to me.

"TO BE OR NOT TO BE"

Somewhere between drink refills at the restaurant, and after overhearing my discussion about the highlights of the real estate seminar, my teenage daughter asked, "Why are you buying this other house? Are we moving into it?"

My wife and I looked at each other a little shocked. Then we realized we had missed an incredible opportunity to teach our kids what we were doing and why. They had certainly realized they had a new set of jobs around the house with my wife's gift basket business, but had gotten no real explanation for it. All of a sudden we were at an important moment: a teaching moment.

After that comment, I truly remembered the rest of that lunch being one of the most rewarding interactions I had ever experienced with my children.

During lunch, it occurred to my wife and me that there was a surprising by-product to this new narrative we had been experiencing the past few months, something we hadn't noticed before. We had talked about teaching the kids to work and writing off expenses related to their services in the business, but we really hadn't included them in the transformation we had been experiencing.

Regrettably, the longer-than-expected lunch was coming to a close, and we needed to rush back to the seminar. My wife winked at me, excited to stay and keep the conversation going as long as she could. I was the one that was actually jealous.

We got back to the classroom just in time for the CPA to lay the groundwork with a diagram he was just starting to discuss. Most CPAs, he explained, discount the benefits of rental real estate because they stay focused on the passive aspect. Apparently the IRS classifies anyone with real estate losses as one of three types of investors. (See Figure 5.2.)

If you are a Passive Investor, you can only deduct passive losses against passive gains. This is the worst place to be as a real estate investor. "A good CPA wants you to have more than that," he said as he raised his fist into the air.

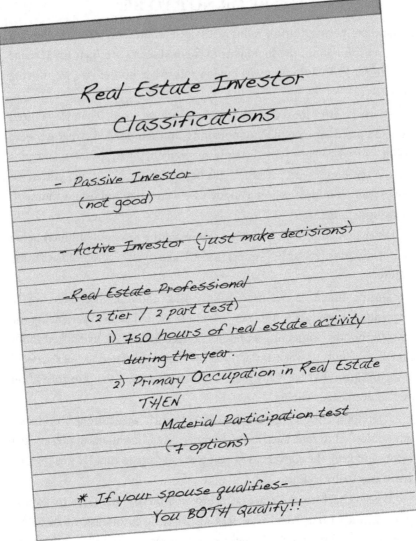

The next investor classification is that of an Active Investor. "This type of taxpayer can deduct up to $25,000 of losses against other income, even if it's a W-2 from a day job," he explained. "The bad news, however, is that it phases out as your income grows. The good news being that it is really easy to qualify for this classification."

I was following him, and I was again surprised my previous CPA never even took the time to explain this principle. The exciting part for the entire class at this point was that even if we phase out, as it's termed, he said we actually don't lose the deductions. We just carry them forward as passive losses and can deduct them in the future when we sell any of our rental properties.

My old CPA would just arbitrarily brush off real estate with the broad statement, "You make too much money." I was excited to find out I could actually use all of those losses/expenses we were keeping track of.

Then with his characteristic comedic timing, the CPA looked in my general direction of the room and said, "But you want more, don't you?" After collaborative nods of heads and some smiles, he retorted, "This is where good CPAs become great CPAs and strategize for their clients."

With everyone on the edge of their seat, we dove into the Real Estate Professional classification.

Apparently, if taxpayers can qualify, they can deduct ALL of their rental real estate losses off against their ordinary income. This was obviously a huge benefit. The CPA went through the numbers on the board.

In order to take these write-offs, however, he explained there was a two-tier analysis. "First, taxpayers must meet a two-part test as a Real Estate Professional: 1) Their primary occupation has to be in the industry of real estate, and 2) The taxpayer must spend at least 750 hours a year in that business of real estate."

He took time to go through some of the details and explain some recent court cases, but most people in the room understood it was reachable and it didn't require taking a test to become a Realtor. Just doing real estate as one's primary occupation was key.

The cool part was when he mentioned, with dramatic antics from the stage, that if one spouse qualifies, then both spouses qualify. My brother-in-law leaned over and said, "This means that all of those rental losses are completely deductible against your corporate W-2 income." I about leapt out of my seat with the realization of what this meant. I immediately thought my wife might have to focus on real estate rather than the gift basket business.

The CPA gave several interesting stories of how one spouse can pay the bills with the day job, and the other spouse can manage the family real estate with a significant impact to the bottom-line tax bill. Interestingly enough, he explained most of his Realtors and contractors were living tax free if they had enough rentals on their books.

Then he joked about the benefits of being married for this strategy, which I thought was a pretty creative twist. I looked at my brother and said, "That perfect tax deduction is out there somewhere." He rolled his eyes.

The second-tier analysis was that of material participation in the rental property. He didn't want to bore us with too much detail and said that he could explain the tests more fully if someone wanted to talk with him afterwards. But essentially there were seven options for qualifying for material participation and a special election had to be made. He said if we were the one primarily responsible for managing your rentals, we should easily qualify.

Bottom line, my brother-in-law and I were high-fiving as we jumped up at the end of the meeting. The power of rental real estate was amazing, but no other CPA had ever explained it in such a manner.

The last words the CPA said that day really stayed with me, "This is why at our office we recommend that every one of our clients purchases at least one rental property a year. Whether they are a plastic surgeon, a dentist, or a truck driver, we want our clients buying a small property each year."

Then in a Shakespearean tone and with his typical antics, he said, "The question then becomes to be or not to be a Real Estate Professional. If it fits your situation for annual tax planning, great, but if not, it's OK. In ten years from now you will still have ten rentals that provide cash flow and a good start on retirement."

I couldn't argue with that, even if I don't like Shakespeare that much.

SUMMARY
Rental Real Estate

Rental property is the most tax-preferred wealth-building technique the average middle-income American can ever utilize. I know this is a bold statement, but I'm convinced this is what your typical financial planner doesn't want you to know and your average CPA neglects to explain.

I recommend that every one of my clients, no matter what walk of life or profession they are in, purchase one rental property a year. Moreover, it can be affordable and relatively easy for anyone to venture into real estate and get the education needed to succeed.

Of course, it almost goes without saying, but I'll say it anyway, that rental property takes some hard work at times and there are risks. However, I want my clients to buy rental property with leverage for cash flow, equity building, and the forced commitment to saving it creates for us.

If you buy rental property simply hoping to obtain appreciation or a fast buck, you will be facing a potential foreclosure like millions did in 2008–2011 for buying unwise property. Get some education on this topic, take baby steps, and don't forget the four major benefits:

1. *Appreciation*. Real estate has averaged more than 6 percent annual appreciation nationwide over the past 70 years.

2. *Mortgage reduction*. If you buy property that at least breaks even with cash flow, the renter is paying the mortgage for you while you get the tax deduction and the equity grows tax deferred.

3. *Tax deductions.* Even if you don't qualify as a Real Estate Professional, all of those expenses you are tracking will still be deductible when you sell the property and continue to build your equity and wealth. In the meantime, even qualifying as an Active Investor may be sufficient.

4. *Cash flow.* Your cash flow can be completely tax free because of the many write-offs, primarily depreciation. In the long run, this is what I want you retiring on as soon as you can afford to do so.

6

LEAVING A
LEGACY

LAW OF THE HARVEST

Now, I certainly realize that not everybody reading my story has children under age 18. But some of you may have kids that still act like they're under age 18, or grandkids, nieces, nephews, siblings, or even adult parents you may be supporting.

Many of you already know there is an epidemic of children flocking back to their childhood homes to live with parents. Some of these children returning home have great college educations but can't find a job, and others could use a little more life training before hitting the road again.

There are a lot of different situations out there, and I mean a lot. However, I am convinced that the concept of small business can provide numerous tangible and intangible benefits to those of us supporting others in our household.

This realization hit me like a ton of bricks during my lunch with my kids during the real estate seminar when they started asking why we were buying another house. What were Mom and I doing, and why? I was almost more excited about my conversation with the kids than about what I had just learned in regards to real estate.

I think men don't embrace the toddler age, the cuteness, the outfits, the diapers, the potty training, etc. Those are the experiences my wife took great pleasure in. She took pictures, recorded measurements, and built an elaborate scrapbook for the kids. I, on the other hand, longed for the day when I could carry on a conversation with them, throw a ball, go to a game, or have some sort of intelligent conversation with them.

It was amazing the discussion we started to have right then and there over French fries and a shake. I felt like Howard Cunningham teaching Richie in an episode of *Happy Days*. Does that date my childhood? Trust me; it was just reruns I was watching.

The beauty was I was actually having an intellectual conversation with my kids about investing and explaining what the American Dream literally was. We talked about the recession, entrepreneurism, and how we, as a family, were going to be changing and seriously embracing this concept. To my utter astonishment, the kids were really excited about it. I was amazed and felt like they were growing up right before my eyes.

Some of you may have these relationships with family members where you provide, provide, provide, and you are lucky to find the rare opportunity to teach them how to take care of themselves. It's awkward at the least, if not impossible, to broach this topic as the recipients get older.

Nevertheless, I think—no, I know—that all of us supporting family members are constantly searching for ways to teach them such principles as self-reliance, money management, and hard work, just to name a few.

This concern even struck more of a chord with my wife. She had actually grown up on a farm. I know that sounds odd to some, but millions of Americans living in the cities and suburbs today grew up in rural areas. They spent their formative years as adolescents and teenagers learning the law of the harvest, as my wife calls it.

I thought that growing up in rural America was cultivating a love of NASCAR and country music. Well, maybe that is a little judgmental. But my wife was convinced that country kids had a better opportunity to learn the concept of hard work and thought city/suburban life wasn't doing us any favors.

Even after all of my blatant remarks and sarcastic undertones, I had to admit she was probably right.

Our kids don't have chores to speak of, no weeds to pull, animals to feed, or garden to water. Sometimes the most our kids have to do is empty the dishwasher once every couple of days.

My wife grew up having to get dirty outside, actually doing jobs that accomplished some meaningful task, and she did some heavy lifting from time to time. Learning to plant a garden taught incredible principles. It took hard work, nothing happened overnight, and there were always variables one couldn't plan for. It was the law of the harvest. We needed to teach our kids these same principles, or at least something remotely similar to them.

So when our new CPA mentioned teaching our kids to work and saving on taxes at the same time, it was like my wife was hearing the message of the gospel for the first time. It was truly spiritual for her. I'm not kidding! She had been praying for ideas on how to better teach our teenagers the concept of work and felt she had received the answer to her prayers.

Of course this whole concept of work is blasphemy or heresy to our children. They questioned her divine revelation as to this need for them to do anything more than fluff the pillows and put the remote on the coffee table after watching TV. That is their idea of heavy lifting.

After a week or two of absorbing this new concept and its impact on our parent-child relationship, my wife sat me down, gave me some notes, and talked me into watching a video regarding Hiring Family Members on our CPA's website.

It was interesting to note that he didn't limit the video to hiring kids. It was actually about any family members or dependents we might be supporting financially.

As I watched the video, I started to have the eerie feeling I was getting a chance to affect my kids in a powerful way. I also got the feeling that I only had one shot at it and had better not screw it up.

To me, the surprising part of the presentation was the list of benefits of hiring a family member. I truly didn't realize how many benefits there were and what the potential could be. Now, of course, my wife and I knew that not every benefit would be realized in our situation, or could be in anyone's situation for that matter. However, it certainly opened our eyes.

I quickly wrote down the list on a pad of paper and considered the different paybacks we might cash in on from having various family members "clock in" to the family business. (See Figure 6.1.)

I was hoping that one of the rewards would be a receiving a hearty thank you when they recognized I was changing their life with this strategy.

However, the CPA dashed my hopes here and reminded us that those little jewels called a "thank you" might not come until many years later.

Oh, well, until then I would just have to hold onto the glimmer of hope that I wouldn't go to my fridge in the middle of the night and find a 20-something child of mine rummaging through my stock of cold cuts.

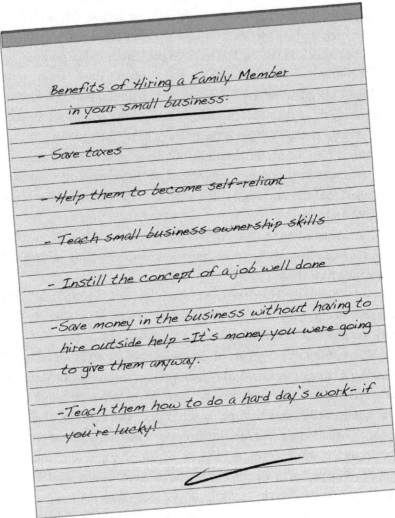

Benefits of Hiring a Family Member in your small business:

- Save taxes

- Help them to become self-reliant

- Teach small business ownership skills

- Instill the concept of a job well done

- Save money in the business without having to hire outside help - It's money you were going to give them anyway.

- Teach them how to do a hard day's work - if you're lucky!

Figure 6.1

LEARNING TO CATCH FISH

The tax savings principle of hiring family members was something the CPA drove home repeatedly in his video. He stated adamantly, "Quit paying taxes and then paying for their stuff, put them on the payroll in your business and let them pay for their own stuff."

I thought about this, and it made complete sense. This is a concept that non-business owner families just don't even think or talk about. Why not get our kids on the payroll and take a write-off?

My wife immediately started speaking with her aunt about her son who was still floundering in his early 30s, still searching for that perfect and always-elusive career. Apparently, her aunt's gift shop venture took place after her son had graduated from high school. Small business was not taught in the home.

My wife and her aunt were now spending hours talking about small business ideas that might pique her son's interest, how they could start creating a business around his strengths and weaknesses almost like a new suit.

I know it sounds presumptuous, and it did to me, too, but what else could her aunt do? She felt like she had failed earlier in life not teaching him a better work ethic and the American Dream. She was excited to maybe have another chance at it and to really help him.

Luckily, with our kids I had the distinct impression I still had a chance. I could hopefully still teach them something!

So when I had that amazing lunch conversation with my kids, my wife took the initiative again to watch some videos and listen to some webinars on the topic from our CPA. Meanwhile, I started having completely new and dynamic conversations with my son and daughter. At least I thought they were dynamic.

During this same period, my son was just starting to drive and my daughter was in her early teens, thinking she deserved to drive given the fact she was, in her opinion, much more mature and talented than her older brother.

It was a great time to have something actually constructive to talk about—a challenge in any parent-teenager relationship. I also began thinking of different jobs each of the kids could do in the business, and my wife was doing the same. It was invigorating for us and terrifying for our children.

Admittedly not all of the discussions with the kids about business and their duties were extremely productive, or even technical, but it certainly gave us a new topic to discuss. I could also start imparting some of my "'wisdom" to the kids.

It was also nice to be teaching them something other than a jump shot or how to chip and putt at the local golf course.

Of course, for those who have older family members struggling to find a job or start a career, why not help them start their own business? It could be better to spend the money to fund the business than to just keep giving them money mindlessly.

With this type of approach, one could create an income for them by teaching them how to catch their own fish, rather than giving them fish. Forgive me for using such an overused quote, but I feel there couldn't be a more appropriate analogy in this situation.

In our little family, we had resorted to buying a family pet to help teach some of these universal laws. However, as all parents know, this is easier said than done. Heaven forbid the kids actually have to feed the damn thing! Many an animal would have ended up at the Humane Society if parents actually waited for their suburban children to clean up after their dog or cat and feed them once in a while.

As I was contemplating the entire notion of small business and family, I found time to watch the video and kept thinking: What can I give my kids to do in the business that is a legitimate job?

Right on cue as usual, our CPA's video dove into this topic. "There are so many things your kids can be doing to help in the business. Let's make a list, and go to the whiteboard." (See Figure 6.2.)

I loved the ideas. I was thinking of a few of my own, and my mind was constantly racing with schemes for my kids.

When brainstorming ideas for hiring children, the CPA reminded us repeatedly in the video, "Make sure that the jobs you give the kids are legitimate and they serve a role in the business. It doesn't have to be an important role, but directly related to the purpose of the business."

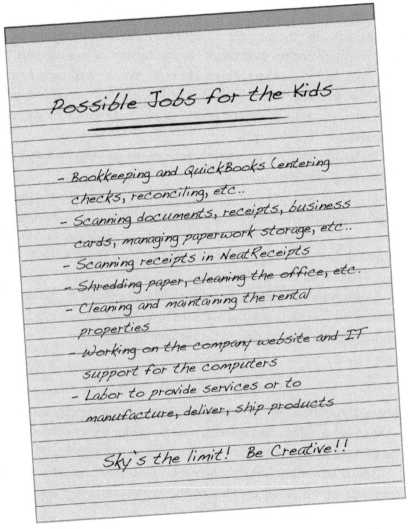

Possible Jobs for the Kids

- Bookkeeping and QuickBooks (entering checks, reconciling, etc..
- Scanning documents, receipts, business cards, managing paperwork storage, etc..
- Scanning receipts in NeatReceipts
- Shredding paper, cleaning the office, etc.
- Cleaning and maintaining the rental properties
- Working on the company website and IT support for the computers
- Labor to provide services or to manufacture, deliver, ship products

Sky's the limit! Be Creative!!

Figure 6.2

He also emphasized that it was important to keep a record of what the kids did in order to withstand an audit if the IRS ever came knocking.

Other than that, it was a green light for my wife and me to start meeting with the kids and giving them new duties and responsibilities. It was certainly a little bit of a headache fitting these new job duties in around schoolwork, but the kids were excited to be earning some of their own money.

We took this time not only to use their earnings to cover expenses we were already paying on their behalf but also to start savings accounts for each child, and to get checkbooks/ATM cards. We required them to give 10 percent to charity and 10 percent to savings each pay period. The bulk of the money was theirs to spend once we covered any out-of-the-ordinary expenses.

It was amazing! We were saving on taxes and teaching the kids some of life's most important principles.

My wife's aunt was trying to do the same with her 30-year-old by helping him start a business. As expected, it was harder than our project. As the old cliché goes, it's difficult to teach an old dog new tricks. Nevertheless, the two of them actually felt they were finally headed in the right direction for once in their relationship.

Her son had always relied on her to bail him out of every financial disaster, but now she finally had a method to hopefully break the cycle. She knew she had been an enabler in the past, but not anymore.

ADOPTING A SYSTEM

Before I could get too far down the path of envisioning a tax-free wonderland and deducting the stuff I was paying for on behalf of my kids, the CPA said there were a few important guidelines to follow.

"First, remember that this is not a sham. We can't put our kid, grandkids, or any family member on the payroll unless they are actually performing bona fide services.

"Second, if your children are over 18, or for other family members, you have to withhold payroll taxes and treat them like any other employee." This payroll procedure can be a pain, he admitted, and told us we should utilize a service to take those headaches and responsibilities over for us.

I thought it might not be worth it if we had to do the payroll thing. Who wants to match Social Security and Medicare? However, the CPA indicated it was all about running the numbers. Putting them on payroll may be worth it if the family member is in a lower tax bracket or no tax bracket at all.

"Third, for those of you with children under age 18, there is a specific procedure that has to be followed, and it can be a huge benefit for family-owned businesses," he explained. "Essentially, for those families you have to pay the kids via a sole proprietorship or an LLC. By doing so you don't have to withhold payroll taxes or FICA." (See Figure 6.3 for an example of a potential structure.)

"Of course, avoiding the payroll procedure is a wonderful bonus, but it only works for your own children or dependents under age 18. It doesn't work for any other family members."

In the same breath the CPA also cautioned us, "Don't pay your kids under age 18 out of your S-Corp or you lose out on the benefit of avoiding payroll taxes on your payments."

Fourth, which adds another layer of fun and savings, is that none of us, including our children, pay taxes on approximately the first $6,000 in income because this is the standard deduction, which is adjusted for inflation every year.

These are funds that become literally tax free. The children can use them to pay for college savings, music lessons, school supplies, private school, sporting goods, food, clothing—the list goes on and on.

"Bottom line," the CPA reminded us in the video, "if you're paying for it, give your kids some jobs in the family business and let them pay for it themselves!

"Now let me tell you the hard part," he cautioned. "You have to take administering the procedure seriously. The trick is having a system that you're dedicated to following, and after that it's a piece of cake!"

You may need to set up a family management company as a Sole Proprietorship to hire the children as a service company.

"However, if you have a rental property and an LLC, it's an even easier fit. The basic responsibility is to keep a separate checkbook for this business and to document the jobs your kids are doing for the business."

The CPA gave us a gentle reminder, as if giving a prescription, "You still need to make sure you have a for-profit business with revenue and

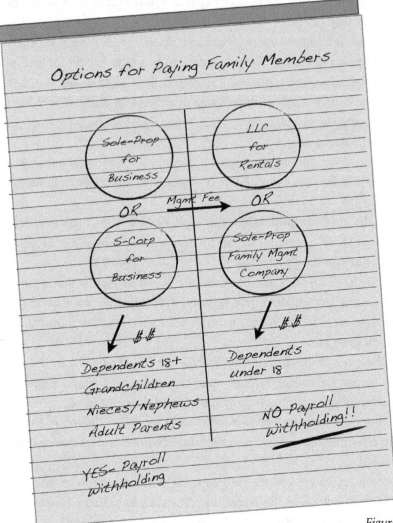

Figure 6.3

you're making a bona fide effort to make the overall system work. Don't forget! The business concept is the foundation of this whole structure and the basis for the payroll procedure."

And just when I thought the presentation was coming to a close, the CPA went to a whole new level that touched both of us deeply. I couldn't believe what we were hearing.

I looked over at my wife, and she was crying. Well, at least her eyes were filled with tears. She said something, but I couldn't understand it.

PERSONAL ACCOUNTABILITY

In the video, the CPA had started out by making the point this can be a win-win. It could help the business owner save taxes, but it could also do something pretty amazing for the family member on the receiving end.

The shocking reality today is that there are millions of adults that are financially dysfunctional. But it's not that easy to simply blame them for not paying attention and learning this in school. Regrettably, fiscal responsibility isn't taught in our schools, at least not at the level most educators and parents wish it could be.

It's not even taught in college, also known as "credit card application heaven." Every college student in America is innundated with enough credit card applications to fill a backpack.

Learning how to manage money requires a set of tools that have to be taught by the family in the home in a consistent, caring, and responsible manner; and it's hard!

However, he said that it didn't need to be as difficult as it seems if we start with the basics. He emphasized how critical it was that family members have their own separate bank account to manage what they receive—even if the money is already earmarked for certain expenses.

The family members need to be cashing their own checks, reconciling their bank account, and paying their own bills. They have to start learning how to manage money.

The CPA went through several examples of how budgeting and spending can be taught within the parameters of the business and the employee relationship we are creating with our family members.

Debit cards, checkbooks, and credit cards need to be introduced at the right time and with the proper education on their use and benefits, as well as their drawbacks and outright dangers.

I was grateful the CPA was encouraging and also understanding about how challenging this process can be. Many of us are poor money managers ourselves, and even the thought of having our own business scares the hell out of us. Nevertheless, with education fear is removed and progress can flourish.

After viewing the video, I admitted to my wife that although the tax savings were going to be sweet, my favorite ancillary benefit was the possibility, just the simple possibility, that our children might learn that financial rewards take time and hard work.

They would start to learn the natural law that plants don't grow overnight, that one needs to tend and care for a garden, seeing it through to the end. The kids also might just learn that they have to follow the laws of integrity, honesty, and patience. They would learn the "Law of the Harvest."

As I looked into my wife's eyes, the I-told-you-so look started to come, and before she could say it, I said, "I guess growing up on the farm wasn't such a bad thing after all." She just rolled her eyes and said, "You're damn right."

She was right, but I was smiling and OK with it. I couldn't believe that tax planning was starting to change our life and soon the lives of our children and extended family.

SUMMARY
Leaving a Legacy

I realize that not everyone has children, grandchildren, or family members they are supporting, but this concept in tax planning and life planning was too important to leave out of this book.

Setting the tax deductions aside for a minute, the benefits of involving your family in your business are simply incredible! Here are just some of the benefits you can pass on to your family and truly leave a legacy that pays dividends for generations to come:

1. *Work ethic in America is at an all-time low.* Children are not being taught the benefits of a job well done. We have to find ways to teach this principle. Why not in your small business?

2. *The American Dream is still alive.* It's on our shoulders to share the passion we have for this dream with our children and teach them about entrepreneurship. It doesn't replace traditional education; it supplements it.

3. *Families in America are getting torn in so many different directions.* With so many extracurricular activities in families, relationships are suffering. Having a small business can create a common project for the family to work on together and rebuild those relationships.

4. *Kids don't need allowances or money given to them.* Earning their own money can empower them and teach financial principles they would never learn in the traditional school setting.

5. *There are also the tax benefits!* We need to quit paying taxes and then paying for our dependent's expenses or giving them money. Put them on the payroll and let them pay their own expenses.

We can legitimately involve family members in our businesses, and the benefits can be astonishing! You don't have to be rich to do this, just change the way you are moving your money.

YOUR
HEALTH CARE

COMMITMENT

It had only been a few months since we first met our new CPA, but we had really committed ourselves to making some changes. We attended several seminars, started networking with other small-business owners and investors, watched a bunch of videos and webinars, and made sure to tell our family and friends about our goals.

We were making progress, even if it appeared slow to outsiders. The biggest changes were in the mental shifts about our future and the way we approached decision making. Our conversations were more long term in nature, but included practical short-term tasks we needed to complete in order to stay on track.

It's true that things were a little overwhelming at times. We looked back at our lives the year before and cherished the memory of how much simpler it seemed. We worked solely for the man and had this blind faith that our 401(k)s and Social Security would take care of us.

Deep down, I think we knew we previously had a false sense of security, but the phrase "ignorance is bliss" is oh, so true. And although I was juggling more, I knew why and felt I was legitimately controlling my own destiny.

Whenever I got discouraged, I would think back to something the CPA said when we left that first Saturday morning seminar, or "our transformation," as my wife called it.

"Don't try to do this all at once," he said. "Just get your business started, set up an entity if it's necessary, begin tracking your expenses, and integrate your family into your project for tax planning."

I also remember his emphasizing a point I took comfort in that gave me confidence that I was truly an entrepreneur: "The most important thing is to make sure your business model is working and you're on track to making money. We aren't doing all of this just to save taxes. We can't let the tax tail wag the dog. Our moneymaking or investment goals are the priority, the tax planning just builds the structure and purpose!"

I felt committed, but as I would soon find out, commitment was something that was running short in my life.

The sense of safety my new plan was giving me soon became more important than ever before, and all of a sudden put more pressure on me to succeed.

One day our office culture had a feeling of positive energy, upward growth, and vision—everything a "lucky" employee has in corporate America today. The next day, however, was not the feeling I wanted to have when going to work. It was also a feeling that many Americans have in corporate America today.

There were problems, as we came to find out. Sales were down. Some subsidiary wasn't doing well. The market shifted. Our parent company needed to make cuts. I don't know which one it really was. It's always a combination of various factors, isn't it?

The result: Our VP in the office called a meeting of the managers, and we were told that the company was going to be split up and the different operations spun off into smaller companies that were to be independent of one another. He explained this meant 401(k) matching was no longer a possibility and health-care benefits were being cut.

Under the new government health-care plan, the new company structure wasn't required to pick up my health insurance. I was now going to have to look at the state insurance exchanges or private insurance.

I remember driving home that day almost in a daze. I was scared and nervous. I thought the company was always going to take care of my benefits. Not anymore.

The word commitment kept coming to mind. I had been loyal to the company. I had been devoted to the Plan. I went to college, got the right degree, went to work for the right company. Why was my life feeling like it was teetering on a precipice? I felt like I was holding on for dear life that night.

I couldn't tell my wife the day it happened. I guess it's a guy thing. I had to hold it in first. Process it. Make sense of all of it. My company wasn't committed to me. At least it felt that way. But should I have been shocked?

Believe it or not, there really isn't some guy at the top sitting in a corner office worried about me. That guy has the same concerns and fears I do. He just works for the Board of Directors and is just as worried as I am about what they might do to him next. Hell, the Directors wonder how long their tenure is going to be, too. They're at the mercy and suffer the temperament of the shareholders.

But who are the shareholders? Guess what? They're you and me! And then the shocking reality hit me personally. I finally realized I wasn't really working for a person or a company. I was working for a system. It was all one vicious cycle.

I have to admit I don't think it's a completely bad system. I'm proud of our country and capitalism. It can do amazing things. However, there are casualties in this type of system, and I had finally become one of those statistics feeling the wrath of market change.

All I remember is that at that point I had the clear and distinct feeling that I wanted to really change my financial equation more than ever. The American Dream I was living was a mirage, and the system could just spit me out at any time.

I didn't want to be spit out.

Commitment. I needed to be committed, but committed to being more self-reliant. I needed that small business or rental property as much as I needed my career. They worked hand in hand.

My stockbroker's comments about being diversified seemed to spill over into every aspect of my life. Damn him for not talking about small business ownership and diversifying my income. All he wanted to do was manage my investments, not guide me to a better future with my day-to-day income.

I knew I needed to make lasting changes, and the rude awakening at the company that week reminded me about the vision I had when I listened to our new CPA. I could do it!

The next day I told my wife about our health insurance problem. She was both scared and nervous. She went through all of the same feelings I did, but with a little more emotion.

What were we going to do without health care? I reminded her we could pay for COBRA for 18 months, and she reminded me how expensive it could be and asked the brutal question, "With what extra money?"

In the past, I hadn't taken much notice of Hillary's efforts to change health care in the '90s, "ObamaCare" in the last decade, or any other effort by the government to change health care. It was too complicated with too many special interest groups controlling the outcome.

Previously I was only concerned about the cost to our growing deficit and what the impact may be on our future generations. Boy, had things changed. Now I had to pay attention more than ever before. I was about to become one of those millions of Americans having to understand my options and figure out how I was going to pay for health care.

After a great deal of discussion, I said to my wife, "I feel we need to make an appointment with our CPA." She said she would call the office and see if we could get in soon or at least have a phone conference.

It's a weird feeling when you are living out a story on the news . . . .

INSURANCE

My wife called to get an appointment, but due to everybody's schedule, a phone conference ended up being the most efficient way to meet.

I started to understand that I had erroneously believed my entire adult life that a face-to-face meeting with my CPA was critical to preparing my tax return or doing planning.

I suppose in today's day and age, technology should also prevail even at my CPAs office. Heck, even the IRS offers online filing, why can't I work with a CPA across the country with e-mail, overnight mail, fax, and phone?

Well, we planned to make sure the kids were busy so we could throw the phone on speaker and talk about the exciting topic of health care.

At first, I thought we were wasting our time talking with a CPA about our health-care woes. Shouldn't we go straight to our insurance agent? So trying to be proactive before our meeting, I dropped by my insurance agent's office. That only added to my discouragement.

My agent was helpful; don't get me wrong. She knew all about the different types of insurance policies available. However, she didn't understand the differences between the FSA/HRA/HSA and which was best for my small business for tax planning.

I had heard of these terms and needed explanations. Ultimately, she said I needed to talk to my CPA. Obviously, all of these issues of insurance and benefit plans needed to be coordinated between my agent and the CPA.

Which one was the best strategy for tax planning? How would it fit into my new business model? How could I reduce my premiums and still get a write-off for the insurance and health care? This was technical knowledge my agent didn't know, or topics that would dramatically affect her commission. I needed an unbiased opinion.

I ultimately realized again that maybe my CPA should be giving me more comprehensive advice than just preparing my tax return and insulting my intelligence for 30 minutes a year.

I was grateful we now had a CPA with a team of planners and not just preparers. Much to our surprise, our telephone call started off with a much broader methodology to our problem than we ever expected.

He made the bold pronouncement at the beginning of the call, "I don't want you to rely on the government or an insurance company for your health care. I want you to self-insure yourselves!

"Now, this doesn't mean I don't want you to take advantage of any government plan, subsidy, or tax policy to enhance your overall plan. We'll exploit any government offering we can to help your situation.

"In fact, we will rely on insurance for catastrophic health-care needs and shop for the most affordable insurance we can for this purpose.

"However, we can self-insure ourselves for all of the smaller health care items, get tax write-offs for all of it, and never again be subject to the whims of an employer or the government."

During these high-level discussion points, my wife and I obviously agreed. Politics aside, we knew we shouldn't or couldn't be relying on the government to make sure we could pay for our prescription drugs next month or even six months from now.

But was it really possible? It seemed too good to be true and a pipe dream to think we could save money, get better tax write-offs, and also get better health care. I covered up the phone and told my wife, "He's lost it! He truly is certifiable. Hurry, hang up the phone!"

My wife just rolled her eyes. I knew he didn't sell insurance, and I certainly didn't want some self-insurance scam promulgated by some incorporation service out of Nevada. I wondered where he was heading with all of this.

"Please hear me out," he urged. "It's really a three-part process to understanding how you can take control of this whole health-care mess. These parts are:

1. What type of insurance plan is best for you in your situation?
2. Which strategy is most effective to write-off my medical expenses?
3. How can I self-insure myself and/or family for future health-care costs?"

Then he cautiously warned us, "This is a lot of information. I'm not going to lie to you. Thus I'm only going to be able to give you the basic outline on this call, but with some education through my written materials and videos, as well as a little bit of personal consultation, you can be off and running.

"When we're finished with the process, you will truly feel that you can literally control your own reality in regards to health care, something millions of Americans are starving for!"

I was spellbound and praying, "Don't let me down, please give me something legit."

He started out explaining step one and the various types of insurance. Of course I wanted to see one of his infamous diagrams. I said I was frustrated with the fact that I couldn't see him up at the whiteboard.

He said, "No problem! We have the technology." I loved it. A nice *Six Million Dollar Man* throwback quote.

He had a cool web service. We just logged onto a website, and he had a virtual whiteboard for us right there on the screen.

He then drew up a diagram showing us the different types of insurance plans we needed to be familiar with. (See Figure 7.1.)

He explained that because it is temporary, the most expensive insurance is COBRA insurance. Second was group insurance because it insures the most unhealthy employee(s) in an organization. This also, of course, tends to be the mainstay of big insurance companies and creates the biggest battles in Congress. Insurance companies love this type of insurance and want everyone on it. It's their most profitable plan.

With persuasiveness and heartfelt concern, our CPA said, "Please don't think you have to have this type of insurance. Too many Americans feel they're a prisoner to their current job because they need the benefits and can't afford to lose them—or so they think.

"Entrepreneurs soon discover that they can create a group of their own if need be, and there are also independent policies if you have the right situation. Believe it or not, independent policies are actually very accessible and affordable.

"Don't feel trapped. My clients soon discover there are more options than they realize."

The main point he wanted to make initially, and be sure we were willing to buy into, was the concept of high-deductible insurance. Even if we were terribly unhealthy, we generally would do better to have a high-deductible plan, reduce our premiums, and use out-of-pocket money for the difference.

I started to understand that saving on premiums and paying out of pocket when and if necessary can truly save thousands.

Now comes the fun part as he termed it. "Saving on insurance premiums is only the beginning. We then want to utilize the right structure

5 General Types of Health Ins.

1. Cobra
- Most expensive
- Temporary
- Only in desperate circumstances

2. Big Company Group Ins.
- 2nd most expensive
- Low-Deductible
- Covers most un-healthy employees

3. Independent Individual Ins.
- 3rd most expensive
- Low-Deductible
- More accessible than people realize

4. High-Deductible Company Group Ins.
- 4th most expensive
- High-Deductible creates lower premium
- Still based on unhealthy
- Allows for HSA

5. High-Deductible Independent Individual Ins.
- Most affordable
- Allows for HSA
- Should always be applied for when searching for Ins. and considered as an option
- Great for the Healthy

Figure 7.1

to save on taxes with our actual out-of-pocket costs and also control the expenses," he said.

Again, another world of planning and savings was opening up right before my eyes. I couldn't wait to hear the rest.

WRITING IT OFF

We then started to dive into the second step in this process and understand which strategy was best to deduct all of this stuff. At first I was shocked to hear the CPA when he said, "About 97 percent of Americans try to write off their health-care expenses as an itemized deduction and phase out. They can't write off their medical expenses!"

I realized the truth of this when I remembered it had actually happened to us. Many newly married couples come to the shocking realization that they can only write off medical expenses over 7.5 percent of their Adjusted Gross Income.

He also explained that this included health insurance expenses. "If you have to pay for your own insurance and don't own a small business, you have a 3 percent chance of writing it off." Fortunately, small-business owners can at least write off all of their medical insurance premiums.

What all this technical jargon means, he said, is "unless you have some sort of broader plan, you're screwed! You can't write off any of your medical expenses or insurance because you make too much money."

We admitted we had given up years ago trying to write off medical expenses and keeping receipts.

He said, "No more! Not you! My clients proactively plan for the right type of health insurance and have at least a small business on the side, and we make sure we write off all of their medical expenses—all of them."

He introduced the next diagram on his cool little computer program, and we watched it right there on our screen. "There are four ways to write off medical expenses. Let's put it in perspective." (See Figure 7.2.)

As usual, this was a lot to digest. He said he had a more detailed summary of each type of plan and would e-mail it to us. We also committed to watch the video he mentioned earlier on this very topic. (A copy of the written summary is in Appendix G.)

The first method that the majority of Americans try to use in writing off their medical expenses is that of the Itemized Deductions; the futile effort we just discussed.

Figure 7.2

He then explained the second most common method in attempting to write off medical expenses was that of the Flexible Spending Account, or FSA. This is the cafeteria plan that millions of Americans use each year to some degree and feel they are doing an excellent job at tax planning. These are also known as use-it-or-lose-it accounts.

Employees can designate a certain amount to be withheld from their paychecks, before taxes, and use the money for a host of out-of-pocket medical expenses. He said emphatically, "Sounds great—except for the lose-it part. Many taxpayers don't use this strategy because they're afraid they won't use the funds and will get stung."

However, he said he told clients who are W-2 employees who have a great health insurance plan and a generous FSA to try to use it as best they can.

The third type of strategy that far fewer Americans are familiar with is the Health Reimbursement Plan or HRA.

Before I could ask what the big difference was, he pointed me to the diagram and the list under the HRA column. "See, this is a reimbursement plan in your business for medical expenses you incur during the year. It's not an account that you lose if you don't spend it, nor does it grow like a Health Savings Account, something we'll talk about in a minute. It is simply a plan to reimburse your employees for all of their medical expenses."

He explained that the HRA is self-administered. You don't need to open an account anywhere, and you don't even have to have health insurance. The critical part, however, is that you had to have a small business operation. Then you could set up a proper structure based on your family situation.

Apparently, your marital status and how many out-of-pocket medical expenses you have dictates in large part how you structure an HRA within your business plan.

My wife then asked the obvious question I was wanting to ask as well, "So when does an HRA make sense?"

He replied with confidence, "Essentially, you need to consider an HRA when you have out-of-pocket medical expenses over and above your insurance premiums of at least $4,000 a year." He added that this was a general figure, but a good benchmark to use when considering which plan is best in your situation.

He explained that the only drawback with an HRA from an implementation standpoint was that it was tricky with an S-Corp but still doable, making the point that again it depends on the individual situation.

He then had us reference various diagrams depicting how the HRA could be structured for married or single taxpayers. (I also included these in Appendix G at the end of this book for your reference.)

The gist of the strategy was first understanding that if you have an S-Corp for ordinary income business planning, the HRA needs to be handled in a separate entity. If you are married, the HRA will be deducted by hiring your spouse in a family management company operated as a Sole Proprietorship. If you don't have an S-Corp, the HRA can easily be included in your Sole Proprietorship without many headaches at all.

When you're single, if you have a large amount of medical expenses, then a C-Corporation may have to be brought into the mix to maximize the medical expense. But again, this is only after a careful financial analysis to make sure it makes sense.

"Bottom line," the CPA said in regards to HRAs, "if we can't write off your medical expenses with an FSA or HSA (discussed below), we'll consider the HRA and run the numbers to see if we should implement one."

At that point, the CPA had to jump off the phone and solve a quick problem. He asked if we could hold for a moment.

While we were on hold, my wife said in a serious tone, "This HRA thing is maybe just what my sister needs." "Your sister?" I said in utter shock.

"Let me explain," she said lovingly.

TAKING CONTROL

We rarely talked about her sister and brother-in-law. They lived across the country, and we weren't really close to them.

Then it hit me. It was a pretty sensitive topic, and I didn't put two and two together at first. My wife's sister had been going through a battle with cancer. They lived in the Midwest, and her husband had been working as a sales rep for a pharmaceutical company.

They thought they had pretty decent health care. Hell, he worked for a company in the health-care industry! However, after surgery and a second round of chemo, their coverage wasn't what they thought it was.

In fact, they had told us in a phone call around the holidays that more than half of the bankruptcies in America were because of medical expenses, and they were people who had health insurance before claiming bankruptcy.

They had told us they were doing all they could do to pay the bills, and on top of that he mentioned they were getting killed with taxes.

Right then a thought occurred to me. I said, "Isn't he a 1099 sales guy for that company he works for?" There was silence for a moment. Then my wife pushed me across the room with excitement in a move that rivaled Elaine on a *Seinfeld* episode. "You're right!" she said.

And then at the same time we both said, "I bet you he doesn't have an S-Corp!" We were both grinning from ear to ear.

Then, with a very serious expression she said, "My sister could really use this information about the HRA."

I returned, "A LOT of people could use this information."

In complete exasperation, I threw my shoe across the room and said, "Why didn't our old CPA or even our insurance agent bring this up before?"

"I don't know," my wife muttered. "Maybe they don't tell us this stuff because they just don't know about it either, or maybe they just don't know how to tell us."

When the CPA got back on the line, we jumped right into the fourth method to write off your medical expenses and also opened up the third step in the overall process: How to self-insure ourselves for years to come. Little did I know that the Health Savings Account or HSA we would discuss next would be completely life changing for us.

"I've heard of this type of account," I commented with excitement. "My brother the chiropractor might have one of these."

With equal enthusiasm he explained, "These HSAs are amazing! Here is the list of things you can do with these:

1. Get a tax deduction on the front page of your tax return that is increased each year for inflation, and it's not an itemized deduction that is limited by your Adjusted Gross Income;

2. A special account is created much like an IRA;

3. You don't lose it if you don't use it;

4. The balance grows tax free from year to year; and

5. I mean tax free! You can pull out money without penalty or tax for a whole list of medical expenses for the rest of your life."

My wife asked with skepticism, "We can actually write off prescription drugs, chiropractic, co-pays, dental, eyeglasses, etc.?"

"Yep," he said, "As a matter of fact you can!"

It was crazy talk I was hearing!

"So what's the catch?" I demanded.

"The only requirement," he said, "is that you have to have one of those high-deductible health insurance plans I talked about earlier. The limits that qualify as a high-deductible plan change each year. Please see my website for the current description of a qualifying plan, but the beauty is how affordable they can be."

So I said, "Essentially what you're doing with these plans is buying catastrophic insurance if your medical expenses go off the chart." No pun intended, I had to add.

"Exactly!" he said. "And then you take the savings from the high-deductible plan and contribute them to your HSA. See, this account is yours to keep for health care for the rest of your life and stays with you wherever you go."

Immediately my wife was a little nervous. She asked, "What if we don't use the HSA for health care, what happens to it?" He explained we shouldn't forget we can use it for long-term care many years from now, but if we don't even use it for that, we can use it like a regular IRA and pull it out under typical IRA rules. Also, if we die, it can be inherited by our spouse or family.

"Unbelievable!" I said, and added, "Why aren't insurance agents selling every one of their clients on these HSAs?"

The CPA wisely explained that HSAs aren't for everyone, and also reminded us to remember the lower-premium aspect of these plans. "Can you figure out why they aren't selling more of these high-deductible policies?" he asked. I just sighed and frowned as I thought about human nature being exemplified to its fullest again.

In a fairly simple-to-understand dialogue, he explained that if you and/or your family are generally healthy, you can be the winners in these plans, not the insurance company.

Instead of overpaying for insurance we don't need, we can take the savings and self-insure ourselves. But the beauty of the whole strategy is that we can then carry around our HSA Visa or MasterCard and pay cash for health-care expenses, including dental, chiropractic, and a host of other expenses.

We now become more engaged than ever before in taking better care of ourselves. We have a renewed interest in preventative health care, and can also negotiate for lower charges because we are paying cash outside of the insurance system.

This entirely new approach can not only drive down our own health-care costs but also eliminate costs that could normally burden the system. The commitment to preventative health-care procedures is the most affordable procedure in health-care systems around the world. We become more motivated to be healthy because we are self-insuring ourselves for the little things.

When we got off of the phone, I think my wife caught the vision of the HSA even more quickly than I did and started to summarize the combination of all of these benefits. It was truly astonishing!

My wife started to think practically about our current situation and exclaimed, "Honey, the awesome part of this is that instead of paying for this expensive COBRA plan your company insurance agent is pushing, we can switch to an independent high-deductible insurance plan and put the savings into our HSA account! We get a tax deduction, and if we don't need the money for the deductible it continues to grow tax free.

"And check this out," she stammered. "We can write off the health insurance premium in my gift-basket business and the contribution to the HSA every year! We are going to save a ton!"

At this point she was hugging me with so much excitement that like any good husband I made an overture for a morning roll in the sack and asked her if we could write off Viagra as well. She immediately said, "Yep, let's go, baby." She wasn't kidding on both counts.

I don't think I could have ever imagined how fun tax planning could be. It was incredible on both counts again!

SUMMARY
Your Health Care

More than ever before in the history of America, we have to be engaged in our health-care planning and understand our options.

Believe it or not, I truly believe we can personally control our health-care costs, find affordable insurance, and write off most, if not all, of our health-care expenses on our tax return.

The two keys to reaching these lofty goals are the use and understanding of Health Reimbursement Arrangements (HRAs) and Health Savings Accounts (HSAs).

The HRA is a plan for those individuals with higher than average medical expenses who also have a small business. It doesn't require an insurance policy, and it's exactly what the name describes: a reimbursement plan where you get to deduct your medical expenses from your small-business profits.

But remember that the structure for the HRA will depend on your family situation and the type of business and entity you have.

Conversely, if you are generally healthy, the HSA is a must. You don't have to have a small business and the ancillary benefit is that you are now paying cash for most of your medical expenses to save money.

The HSA is a fantastic structure that actually forces you to get a high-deductible insurance policy, which then allows you to make tax-deductible contributions into an account you can build tax free. Then at any time in the future, you can pull out tax-free amounts for medical expenses the rest of your life.

Bottom line, if you are willing to engage in the discussion and get a little bit of education on the topic, the rewards can be amazing. I have had countless students and clients save thousands of dollars with a little proactive health-care planning.

See Appendix G for more detailed explanations of the FSA, HRA, HSA, and additional diagrams.

CONCEPT

8

DISCOVERING
PLUTONIUM

THE SHOCKING REALITY

Well, my brother and I followed the procedure and method we learned for locating and purchasing a quality investment property. It took a couple of months, and although we hoped for a fix-and-flip, we couldn't find the buyer we wanted yet.

Of course, the good news was that our fall-back strategy of a rental was working well. Because we were able to get it at a lower price, the carrying cost to rental income was really paying off.

I was also still plugging along with my career, or day job, and the balance was comforting. I knew I had something someday I could fall back on if I needed to, and the extra cash was going to be nice along the way.

My wife's new business was also doing well, and she was completely energized with the process. She loved her newfound identity as a business owner, and her friends were enthralled with her experiences. It seemed that's all they talked about, rather than their husbands' lackluster home repair skills.

Everything seemed to be going pretty well. Too good to be true as the cliché goes. Something was about to rock our world.

The call came to my office on a busy afternoon. My wife was in tears on the phone, and I could barely understand her. My first reaction was the kids, of course. "Are they OK? What happened? Who got hurt?"

You know the sickening feeling in your gut, when words seem to just rattle off the tip of your tongue faster than you can think.

The kids were fine, thank heavens, but her father had suffered a severe heart attack while he was jogging that day. After being rushed to the hospital, he had died.

It was surreal. One of those times where you remember exactly where you were and what you were doing when you heard the news. For example, I even remember what music was playing in the background and the smells and sounds the day my wife was in a car accident years earlier. You never forget that stuff.

He was only in his early 60s, and we had just played golf together a month ago. I remember really enjoying our conversation as I was explaining his daughter's new business to him and some of the things we were doing. He mentioned regretting that he had not taught his kids more of those concepts earlier in his life and hinted at some interesting business experiences of his own.

I was intrigued and wanted to learn more about his comments. I planned on doing so, but it was not to be.

It was surprising how supportive of us he was. He was a corporate man through and through. He was so proud of me when I got my most recent job in middle management and it seemed I was on the fast track to higher positions.

The next few weeks went by quickly. He and Mom lived close to us, so we were the primary ones to help with the funeral arrangements. My wife took it pretty well after the initial shock. It's funny how life takes you around corners and down paths you didn't expect, or at least expect to face at that time.

During the process we made an appointment with our business/ estate planning attorney to get our estate plan finished. It was something we had put off way too long. I suppose the whole affair was a wake-up call of sorts.

It was only a month or so after his passing, and shouldn't have been a surprise, but my mother-in-law called me one day confused and frustrated about her finances. The surprise was not that she called me; it was the awkward realization this was now my station in life.

I felt I was capable enough of helping her, but realized that I was growing up again and handling the affairs of my parents had come much sooner than I expected.

My wife and I went over to meet with her that evening and lay out all of the mail on the kitchen table in order to figure out what was going on. Mom was finally emotionally ready to deal with it.

The life insurance made sense; it wasn't too difficult. It was tax free and paid directly to Mom. We just needed to make some phone calls and follow up with forms and a death certificate. The cars and the house were manageable, too.

There was no estate tax at this point because Dad left everything to Mom. However, the estate planning attorney had told her there were issues that needed to be dealt with in the near future. If something happened to her, there could be serious estate tax problems.

But then the retirement plan statements started to pile up on the corner of the kitchen table. Too many options: roll over, transfer, distribution. Which option was best?

Shockingly, I thought he had more in his company 401(k). As I was going through the statements, it hit me. I had to get my house in order to make sure my retirement was being built more effectively and quickly.

We were starting a small business and buying a little real estate. It was a lot more than we were doing 12 months earlier, but would it be enough?

It was alarming to see the infamous 401(k) at work. This is when it was supposed to pay off, right? My father-in-law had worked for years and years, contributing to his 401(k) religiously. "Yes, I'll get matching and do my maximum contribution." I'm sure that's what he said. We all say it.

Be a good corporate employee. It's what we're taught in the financial magazines funded by the Wall Street machine. Fall in line.

His 401(k) was not anywhere near where I thought it should have been. I was always impressed with his frugality, and he had done well with his company. He had retired right on time and with honors. He got the gold watch.

Obviously it's better than simply relying on Social Security. Heaven forbid that was all Mom had to retire on. But damn it! There should have been more in his 401(k) after all of those years. I should have more in my 401(k)!

I couldn't say what I was feeling out loud. Mom was under enough stress. However, I think she was thinking the same thing.

At that point something happened that would turn out to be the most influential lesson I would learn the entire year.

Ironically, I noticed one of my father-in-law's IRA accounts that was outside of his company retirement plan. It far exceeded the balance in his 401(k). I set it aside on the other corner of the table and thought it must be an old IRA rollover or something from an earlier 401(k) in his career. But as I kept coming back to it and asking Mom about the details, she would just explain it away as Dad's little investment account and brush it off.

While I was trying to pry any facts I could out of Mom regarding this little account, it was becoming more and more apparent that we were in a little over our heads in regard to this unique retirement plan. What were the elections and options before us? We were going to need some tax and financial advice.

This is also the point when my wife could tell Mom was at a breaking point for the evening. The stress of the situation was getting a little much. Without even looking at me for my thoughts or comments, my wife started telling Mom about this CPA we know who will give her straight answers, and if he doesn't know exactly what to do, he will find the answers.

Apparently my wife had said the magic words. Mom was immediately thrilled to hear we had a resource. She and my father-in-law had really not fostered a strong relationship with their CPA, and Mom hadn't known whom to call.

Clearly his other account was a mystery, at least to my wife and me, and it was obvious Mom wasn't going to talk to us about it.

Maybe our CPA could play a little Magnum P.I. with Mom and figure this thing out. Mom was certainly hiding something, and hopefully it wouldn't take a red Ferrari and a well-endowed mustache to make her spill the beans.

WHAT WALL STREET DOESN'T WANT
YOU TO KNOW

It had been about nine or ten months since our first meeting with our CPA, and it was nice to be back at his office. I always learned something new when we met. However, today I was just expecting to get Dad's affairs in order and get to the bottom of his secret account. Little did I know I was about to learn the most amazing principle yet in building my wealth.

After the usual greetings and taking our seats at the conference table, we laid out all of Dad's documents. We started going over our list of questions about the 401(k). Interestingly enough, the CPA honed in on the other account much quicker than I expected. He wanted to get the big picture of all of the assets before recommending the best course of action for the 401(k). It made sense.

He asked Mom direct questions about where it had originated. My wife and I had surmised that it was some old IRA with a stockbroker we didn't know about.

With some investigative prodding from the CPA, Mom told us that Dad would do some lending out of it. "Lending?" I said. "What kind of lending?" I was starting to wonder if he had a loan sharking business he was running for some Italian family in New Jersey with a last name similar to that of the Sopranos.

Mom finally started to confess when I focused one of the desk lamps at her from the table in the corner. Well, maybe I didn't have to pull an FBI move on her, but it felt like it. She started to speak under her breath, "Well, Dad and I would make what he called hard money loans for investors or small-business owners from time to time over the past ten years."

My wife and I looked at each other in shock and with smiles. Come to find out, this whole time Dad been lending money in legitimate ways, almost like a small business on the side while playing the follow-the-line company man. "Amazing!" I congratulated her. Mom was surprised I was commenting with such approval.

As we talked with her, we discovered that she thought they were a little crazy for carrying on this little investment strategy when their stockbroker would have never approved. "It was always, mutual fund this, bond ladder that, and maybe an annuity for good measure," she said.

"Your Dad and I had a little money from an IRA early in our marriage and thought this was something we could do to get a better return rather than entrusting the IRA to the stock market."

She starting pulling out files from her bag, and I was poring over them smiling, shaking my head over and over again in disbelief. I didn't think it was possible to do such a thing in an IRA and asked Mom if she knew what Dad had been doing. I hinted that he had probably done something illegal and the IRS was wire tapping the conversation.

At that moment the CPA alarmed all of us and started giving Mom high-fives across the table and congratulating her for the wisdom she and Dad displayed over the years.

Sheepishly, Mom admitted she didn't know too much about what Dad had been doing with the IRA, but said he would tell her from time to time how excited he was about the project.

Our CPA was ecstatic with this news and assured us that Dad had not done anything illegal. In fact, he said, "Your husband was implementing a strategy I have been teaching my clients since I opened my practice ten years ago, but he was on to it much sooner than that. When did he learn about self-directing his retirement plan?"

Mom explained she didn't know it was such a groundbreaking concept, let alone where Dad had learned about it.

The CPA was able to figure out that Dad started doing 15 years ago what millions of Americans are rushing to do in the market today. That is the art of self-directing their retirement plan with alternative investments such as lending, real estate, and small-business ventures. They are fleeing the stock market in the droves.

He announced with his characteristic enthusiasm that Dad had built up more money in this old IRA in a fourth of the time it would have taken him to do so with his measly retirement plan at work with the company's generous matching program.

I have to admit I was a little bugged and asked him when he had planned to tell us about this relatively unknown strategy and why this was news to my wife and me.

The CPA explained this education was certainly on its way, and he was simply bringing us along in baby steps. He also reminded us that we had really only been working together for less than a year.

I agreed and was actually grateful he hadn't overwhelmed us with too many strategies too quickly.

The CPA then went on to explain the best-kept secret I had ever heard. A secret Wall Street is loathe to sell or mention to its clients.

Mom was all ears and was thrilled to finally understand what this account meant to her and her financial future.

With his typical candor and simple explanation, the CPA said, "The strategy is called self-directing your retirement account. Most financial magazines, papers, and talking heads on the major networks completely downplay or discourage it."

He was right! I had heard rumblings of this concept at work and in some news commentaries, but the general gist of it was that you should never trust yourself to invest your own retirement plan. You and I aren't smart enough. Let your financial planner handle your account.

Essentially, when you self-direct, you transfer your funds (tax free) to a self-directed custodian and by doing so fire your current stockbroker. You're now free to invest your account as you see fit so long as you follow some prohibited transaction rules to make sure you don't run afoul of the IRS or Department of Labor.

The CPA was also quick to point out that some financial planning firms have aligned themselves with self-directed custodians in order to provide this service, but it is certainly the exception and not the norm. He urged me to talk with my current financial planner and see if his company provides this option.

He also smiled and said, "Remember, allowing you to day trade your IRA online with various mutual funds or stocks is NOT self-directing. Make sure you indicate you want to buy real estate, buy tax liens, or invest in LLCs, just to name a few, and see what they say."

When I realized that I could invest in projects that might give me a higher return than the standard S&P 500 index and, most importantly, that those investments would grow tax deferred OR tax free in a ROTH format, I was completely blown away.

My entire perception of investing my retirement plan was changing at light speed. It was as if I was discovering plutonium!

We then dove into some of the rules and options when investing a retirement plan.

THE DOS AND DON'TS

Many times my friends or I would ask our financial planner or stockbroker about creative ideas for investing. The typical answer was that it was prohibited to pull the money out for that type of investment without penalties, or we can't do that inside a retirement plan.

The concept or option of self-directing was never mentioned, let alone encouraged. The reality was that it wasn't that we couldn't do the investment, it was that they couldn't do it at their brokerage firm. I had literally been lied to.

My mother-in-law, wife, and I then spent the next hour talking with our CPA about the rules and guidelines for self-directing. It was true that managing your own retirement plan wasn't for everyone. In fact, the CPA was still an ardent supporter of being well diversified and using caution while investing.

"However," he said as he almost pounded on the table making his point, "if you know how to invest your money in something you know better than the stock market, don't you think it's wise to take some money in your retirement plan and invest it in something you know best? Absolutely. It's your money!"

In typical fashion, he then pulled out a yellow pad and started listing what we could DO and then what we could NOT DO (Figure 8.1).

As he summarized this list, he made a point that I thought was extremely wise. "The first step is to decide what you want to invest in. Don't start moving money to a new self-directed custodian without an end in mind. Knowing what you want to invest in and how you are going to fund it in the short and long term will dictate the type of procedure you will follow and what structures you may need."

The next thing he emphasized was to have an attorney working with you—an attorney that was on the same page with your CPA. IF there is

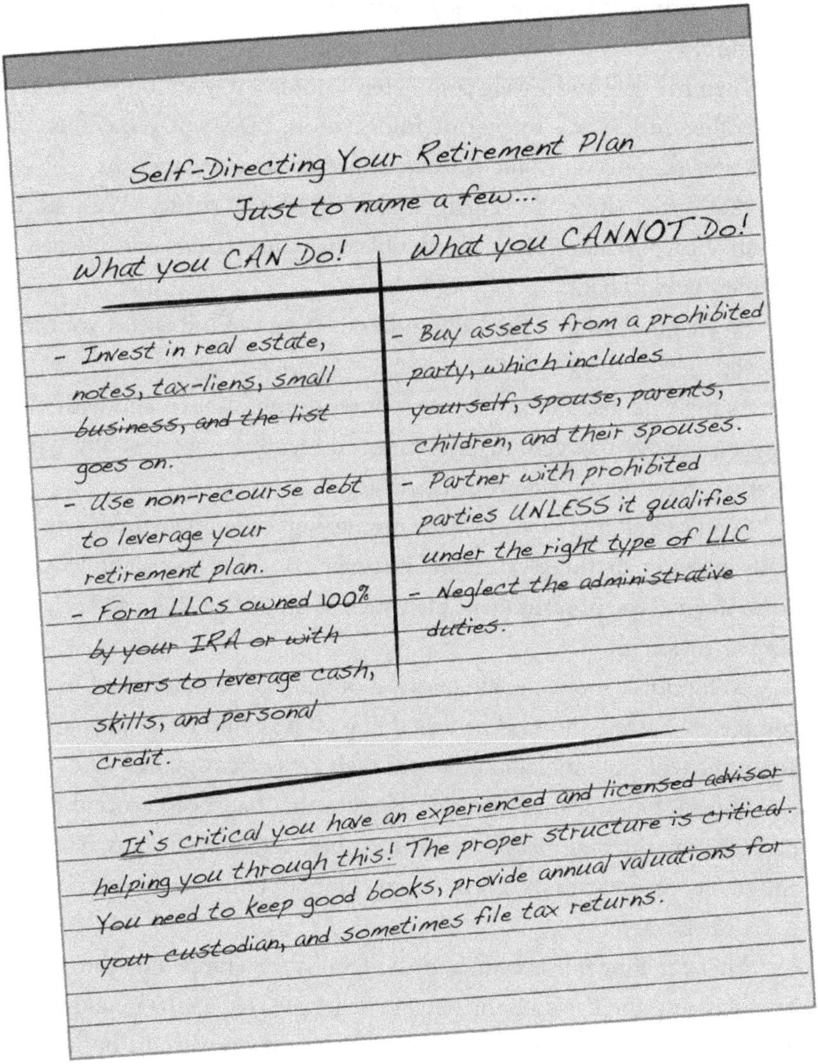

Self-Directing Your Retirement Plan
Just to name a few...

What you CAN Do!	What you CANNOT Do!
- Invest in real estate, notes, tax-liens, small business, and the list goes on.	- Buy assets from a prohibited party, which includes yourself, spouse, parents, children, and their spouses.
- Use non-recourse debt to leverage your retirement plan.	- Partner with prohibited parties UNLESS it qualifies under the right type of LLC
- Form LLCs owned 100% by your IRA or with others to leverage cash, skills, and personal credit.	- Neglect the administrative duties.

It's critical you have an experienced and licensed advisor helping you through this! The proper structure is critical. You need to keep good books, provide annual valuations for your custodian, and sometimes file tax returns.

Figure 8.1

an LLC used in your structure or investment, it is absolutely essential that the attorney understands ERISA, IRS, and DOL rules regarding retirement plan investments and designs the Operating Agreement.

Apparently, these types of LLCs are not boilerplate documents, and our CPA or an incorporation service should not be designing these documents. We need them tailored to our situation with a comfort letter regarding the procedures we will need to follow particular to our structure.

Then my wife and I were completely astonished when our CPA threw in another little juicy nugget of information. "Do you remember that Health Savings Account, the HSA we talked about a few months ago?"

"Yes!" my wife said excitedly and with a bit of pride. "We took the initiative to purchase a high-deductible insurance policy and opened an HSA at the local bank!"

"Well, guess what?" the CPA smirked. "You can self-direct your HSA as well."

As my wife and I looked at each other dumbfounded and with blank stares, he said, "You can buy real estate, do lending, or most any type of creative investment inside your HSA!"

"You're kidding!" I said. "This is amazing!" We learned that you can really invest in anything except life insurance or collectibles, and we could do so in any type of retirement plan such as an IRA, 401(k), ROTH, SEP, Simple, or Keogh.

"Why don't more people know about this?" I implored of him. He completely agreed and said he was doing all he could to let people know about the true potential and power of their retirement plans.

Indeed, he said, there were companies that had been around for the past 30 years helping people self-direct their retirement plans. They just couldn't compete with the big brokerages for Super Bowl commercial time.

Unbelievable!

After catching our breath, almost literally, we wrapped up the meeting by discussing the basic alternatives to roll over Dad's 401(k) and IRA. It was pretty simple stuff, but even Mom was energized with the options that now lay before her for investing and building her overall retirement. After all, she could easily have 20-plus years in front of her and needed to keep her money working.

She was soaking this up, but I was still a little startled that she had tears in her eyes when she looked over at my wife and I and said, "I am so grateful to your father for being such a visionary and wise enough to take advantage of this strategy years ago."

Then as good mothers do, she counseled us, "Don't take this knowledge for granted. Your retirement years will be here before you know it."

As we started putting the papers together on the table and heading toward the door, the CPA said there was one more piece of information that would simply astonish us.

"Many people don't realize that retirement plans are almost completely asset protected," he said. "In almost any potential lawsuit, a plaintiff or creditor cannot touch your retirement plan."

He started to joke and stressed this point with an example of O.J. Simpson. I thought back to all of the drama of O.J.'s trial, move to Florida, book writing, and ultimate Vegas hotel break-in. The entire time he had been living on his NFL retirement, completely protected from those lawsuits. It was true! He had kept his retirement income the entire time.

When I realized what he was explaining, I exclaimed with excitement, "So Mom and Dad not only saved taxes all these years while building their wealth, these assets were also completely protected. Even if she got in a horrific car accident, she would still have her retirement paying her dividends the rest of her life?"

"Yep," the CPA said matter-of-factly, with a big smile.

My wife and I just stared at each other with a somber nod of gratitude and amazement. We had truly discovered plutonium and a strategy that would change our lives permanently.

SUMMARY
Discovering Plutonium

The concept of self-directing is exactly what Wall Street doesn't want you to know about; and if you do find out about it and ask questions, they are quick to remind you that you have no business managing your sacred retirement account. You'll just lose it.

On the other hand, I'm convinced this is a cornerstone concept in regards to your retirement planning. Who would have thought that you, of all people, should have the audacity to decide what you think is best for your retirement plan?

Now, I'm not saying that diversity in your retirement plan isn't important. Nor am I saying that you shouldn't have a portion of your assets in traditional market securities, equities, mutual funds, or bonds, but for heaven's sake, can't you put some of your retirement plan into what you know best?

Purchasing real estate, lending, small business, and all sorts of investments are fair game for your retirement plan. Yes, you will have to involve an attorney and/or CPA in the planning process to make sure you avoid prohibited transactions, but it is certainly doable.

Moreover, the tax benefits of funding a properly designed retirement plan aren't discussed anywhere nearly enough by CPAs and their clients. The stock answer is to simply open an IRA. We need to be shifting our income to our retirement plans and using our small-business projects to fund them. We need to shift our mentality.

Finally, don't forget that retirement plans are completely asset protected, as I discuss in my book *Lawyers Are Liars—The Truth About Protecting Our Assets* (Life's Plan Publishing, 2007). No one can touch your retirement plan in almost any situation. Just ask O.J. Simpson: He'll tell you how he's got the sweetest retirement plan in cell block D.

The power of a well-designed retirement plan just gets better and better!

MY
RESOLUTION

As the months passed by, I felt young again. The grass looked greener. Life was more precious. I know that sounds ridiculous. But I truly felt I was in more control of my destiny than ever before in my life.

I still work a corporate job. I haven't thrown away my career. But I am also now an entrepreneur. I am more educated than before.

I don't know how things are going to turn out. Maybe good, maybe bad. But I no longer feel that my financial life is in someone else's hands.

My wife is still doing gift baskets, but primarily managing our real estate. We now have a couple of rental properties and a little fixer-upper that we are working on with the kids on weekends and plan to focus on in the summer.

Thank heavens they wouldn't be working at a fast food restaurant or sitting around the house playing video games. They will be working for my wife and me, in our business, by our side.

If we break even on the sale of the fix-up, we would count it a winner. We still will have taught some work ethic to our kids, spent time together as a family, and hopefully learned a little something along the way.

If we make money on it, the profits will go directly into college savings for the kids and a good piece of it in their tax bracket. It is their project, too, and we would be excited to see them succeed.

They are still going to go to college. However, I sometimes have the feeling they are learning more with my wife and me about business and life than they will learn someday in a textbook at the university. I knew they need both aspects, and I am grateful to have discovered the missing link.

Meanwhile, my wife's gift basket business is like millions of other small businesses that people are working hard at every day across America. It isn't easy, but they know it's theirs. Theirs to make it big or lose big, but in the end, they control their own destiny and know it.

Call it capitalism, commercialism, or simply entrepreneurship. It's the American way. When our ancestors came to America hundreds of years ago, they embraced the same spirit that we can still live today. There are few places in the world that afford us this opportunity, love or hate the politics of it.

I'm still surprised that I discovered all of this when discussing the biggest expense in my life—taxes, the very process and transaction that supports the government, which in turn protects our freedom to live the American Dream.

We may complain about taxes, but most Americans really don't talk about saving money here in meaningful ways with CPAs that understand the Code. We think do-it-yourself software has filled our empty feelings of apathy and discouragement. However, we can't just do it ourselves. We have to involve a CPA to really save.

It's a fair argument that we should be able to do our taxes without a professional. It shouldn't be that complicated. But it is. Ignoring that fact ultimately only costs us.

The opportunities are too great, and the mysteries that can be unfolded through the confident and proactive teaching of a CPA are astonishing.

May more of our CPAs catch the vision of the power they can share to change lives, and may we be more apt to listen.

Most CPAs really want to tell us these secrets, they just don't know how. And, unfortunately, we don't ask.

My Resolution

ADDITIONAL
RESOURCES

Appendix A. Bookkeeping Basics to Save Time and Money

Appendix B. The Best Business Entity When It Comes to Taxes

Appendix C. The C-Corp vs. S-Corp Debate—Who Wins?

Appendix D. The Business Plan

Appendix E. A Dynamic Strategic Plan

Appendix F. The *Perfect* Marketing Plan

Appendix G. Selecting the Best Health-Care Strategy to Save Taxes

Appendix H. The Strategic CPA

Appendix I. Maximizing Write-Offs: A List You Have to Have!

APPENDIX A

Bookkeeping Basics to Save Time and Money

Almost every small-business owner sees bookkeeping as either a burden that sucks up unnecessary time or an intimidating topic, where they always second-guess their procedures.

Thankfully, that doesn't have to be the case. Successful business owners don't view bookkeeping in this way because they have adopted a few basic procedures to stay on top of the paperwork. By doing so they undoubtedly save time and money. Consider the following and the impact they can have on your business:

1. Immediately get QuickBooks® installed on a computer dedicated to bookkeeping. Become at least generally familiar with the software, that is, know how to input checks, reconcile bank accounts, print out reports, etc. Then decide on one of the five ways to maintain it:

   A. Do it yourself and dedicate at least one day a week to input information and reconcile your bank information. Commit yourself to taking a class on QuickBooks and stay on top of the bank statements. If you let the transactional input get behind, it can be difficult to tackle it. This is when most people throw all of the bank statements into a pile on a shelf and procrastinate. If this happens, you'll usually end up with Option E below.

   B. Train and hire one of your family members to do the regular procedures of maintaining the books. Have a computer devoted to bookkeeping that he can access whenever necessary to operate QuickBooks. Remember, it's still important that you have at least a basic working knowledge of the software program and the procedures. From a supervisory role and internal control system standpoint, this is critical.

C. Hire a local college student that needs school credit in accounting and knows QuickBooks. You will typically find these students to be very affordable per hour. You can also schedule the student for specific times during the week and maybe even share them with other business partners you may have. Just remember not to give the student too much latitude with check signing or control of paying bills. Although the student is running the system, you still need to stay on top to make sure your books are tight.

D. Hire a local bookkeeper to provide the services you need, and turn the books over to your CPA for planning and tax preparation at the end of the year. You are certainly going to get a higher-quality person with a strong knowledge of QuickBooks. However, the cost per hour is going to go up. A strategy that works well in this area is to have a fixed monthly fee so you can budget for the service.

E. Your final option, and typically what happens when your books have been a mess all year, is you engage your CPA to provide bookkeeping services in conjunction with the tax return prep at the end of the year. At first blush this can seem to be the most expensive of the options. However, your CPA team will probably be the most skilled and be able to complete the work quickly and efficiently. Thus, even though the hourly rates are higher, the fee should be similar to what you would have paid a bookkeeper during the year to do it on a monthly basis. In fact, you could engage your CPA to do monthly or quarterly reports to stay on top of things. The benefit of using your CPA exclusively is that you can usually have confidence it was done right.

Bottom line, if you don't want to end up with Option E, choose one of the others and make it happen. But no matter what, don't ignore the bookkeeping. Avoiding the bookkeeping is the most expensive option of all. You will lose out on deductions you would have captured with a uniform system.

2. Consider using NeatReceipts© to scan in your receipts, business cards of contacts, and other important items. It imports directly into QuickBooks, saves tons of time, and helps audit-proof your records, not to mention saves paper. This is also an excellent procedure to give one of your family members if you are using the strategy of putting family on the payroll. Give them an inbox for receipts, and ask them to regularly scan them and organize your paperwork to go paperless. Again, this can save you time and money by avoiding lost deductions at the end of the year or a potential audit.

3. Maintain separate credit cards for each business operation and, of course, your personal expenses. It will make bookkeeping much, much easier and also help maintain your corporate veil (if you have a formal entity). When you commingle credit cards with personal and business expenses, it makes the goal of maximizing your tax write-offs almost impossible. Help your CPA save you money by keeping things separate and organized in categories.

4. Maintain separate checking accounts. Keep your checkbooks separate between different business entities, operations, and your personal expenses. Don't commingle, and try not to use cash. Use your debit card religiously. When you use cash you lose track of potential write-offs. If you have to pull money out of an ATM, at least make a note on the ATM receipt as to what the cash will be used for.

5. Keep a file on each piece of real estate you purchase, whether it's your home or rental property. Keep everything: the settlement statement, mortgage documents, appraisal documents, inspection documents, etc. You never know when these records will be important from a tax or legal (lawsuits) perspective. Six years after you sell a property, you can get rid of the records. See the next item.

6. Hold on to all tax records for at least six years and consider going paperless in the process. Storing that much paper can be daunting to say the least. I recommend all my clients to consider purchasing a small fireproof safe. You need one for your passport, life insurance

policies, and numerous other important documents anyway. With the safe ready and available, you can create a backup of your bookkeeping software regularly and your tax returns, and save them on a flash drive. You may also want to consider off-site storage for your records and scanned files. There are plenty of great websites that provide this service.

7. Make sure to implement some sort of procedure to track your auto mileage. Trying to keep a written record of business, charitable, and medical mileage can be difficult at best. Look into a satellite-assisted service, phone application, or software program. New ones are coming out all of the time, and with a little bit of homework you will find one that fits your style.

8. Finally, commit to meeting with your CPA at least once every six months for at least a few minutes to review your business plans, financials, tax deposit amounts, payroll procedures, tax strategies, etc. The cost of taxes is just too high to leave your plans to chance. Just a few minutes on a regular basis can save thousands. Also, remember that your CPA should be bringing you strategies and ideas in these meetings. If the meeting consists of you throwing out ideas and your CPA shooting them down, you have the wrong CPA. Get a planner that is reaching out to you with ideas and strategies on a regular basis.

APPENDIX B

The Best Business Entity When It Comes to Taxes

I realize that many of you may find this whole topic of entity selection either too boring, overly complex, or one you already have a handle on.

As I presented in the preceding story, however, there are various issues and factors to consider when choosing your form of doing business, especially from a tax perspective. Many of the differences between the forms of doing business come down to tax issues.

It was difficult to explain many of the pros and cons of each type of entity in the context of the story, so I am including this section to give you what I feel to be absolutely critical information for the small-business owner.

So many business owners make the wrong choice in this area of their business planning, and it costs them dearly later on in time and money. PLEASE don't rely on what your friend suggests, a family member's advice, or, most importantly, a non-licensed "advisor" that accuses lawyers of being liars and CPAs of being too conservative or out of touch with on-the-street strategies.

I STRONGLY encourage you to know the basics and then consult with your CPA and attorney to decide on the correct business entity given your situation. It's not too much to ask to get these two folks on the same page with your small-business goals.

The following is what I consider to be the TRUTH about the five forms of doing business:

1. Sole Proprietorship
2. C-Corporation

3. S-Corporation
4. Limited Liability Company (LLC)
5. Limited Partnership (LP)

Sole Proprietorship

The Sole Proprietorship is really not an "entity" per se; yet interestingly, it is the most common form of doing business in America. But just because it is the most popular, doesn't mean it's the best choice for everyone.

The reality is that there are very distinct pros and cons of operating under this form. Most business owners simply "fall" into doing business as a Sole Proprietor because it is so cheap and easy. Anyone can literally open a personal lemonade stand up tomorrow and become a sole proprietor. It's the American way!

The Benefits

As I said above, the Sole Proprietorship is simple and affordable to form. It occurs literally by default if you don't actively form an entity with the state. You are in startup mode the moment you start incurring expenses and officially "in business" once you make that first sale. There is no formal filing required with a city, county, or state. In fact, you can use your own Social Security number and don't need federal or state tax ID numbers unless you are going to have payroll or sales tax filings.

The Drawbacks

There are essentially three major problems with sole proprietorships: exposure to liability, the self-employment tax (SE tax), and audit risk.

This is not a book about asset protection, but most everyone knows that your personal assets are completely exposed when operating your business as a Sole Proprietorship. I suggest you read my book *Lawyers Are Liars—The Truth About Protecting Our Assets* for an explanation of what really works in asset protection and scams to avoid.

The second drawback is the SE tax that blindsides many, many Sole Proprietors. This is a tax of 15.3 percent on the net income of your business. It is actually 15.3 percent on the first approximate $100,000 (this threshold amount is adjusted yearly based on inflation) and then 2.9 percent on everything above that amount. Also, it's important to note that the actual rate of tax may also vary with special legislation from time to time. But no matter what the rate is, far too many small-business owners overpay this tax.

Therefore, it's important for Sole Proprietors to maximize all of their expenses to keep their income down and to monitor their net-income levels to make sure they convert to an S-Corporation when the time is right (see the S-Corporation discussion below). Figure B.1 is a diagram of how the dreaded SE Tax can add up so quickly.

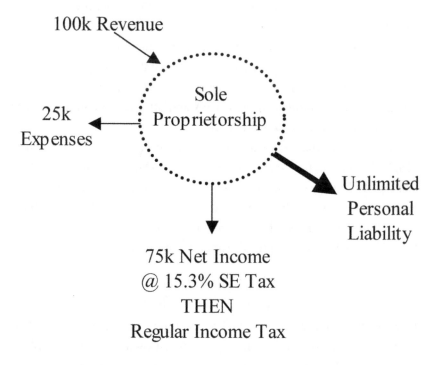

Figure B.1: Sole Proprietorship for Operations

The third problem with Sole Proprietorships is that they are the most likely to be audited by the IRS. Historically, they have been audited more frequently than any other form of doing business. If I have clients that are more aggressive with their tax write-offs, I recommend they consider operating under a different form of doing business simply for the purpose of significantly reducing their chances of an audit.

When Do They Make Sense

There are two primary instances where operating as a Sole Proprietorship may be a smart choice for you to consider.

First, if you are just getting started with a business concept, a Sole Proprietorship may be a great fit for you. You might be selling something on the web or just developing your product or service and really aren't in full operation yet. I think it can be overkill to set up a formal company when your company is in its infancy and you aren't yet sure if you're going to follow through with the concept.

However, once you are committed to the project and liability protection becomes a concern (as with a rental property) or you are starting to make 20K+ a year in net income (thus your SE Tax bill is starting to rise), consult with your CPA and attorney to consider which entity is best for you in your situation.

The second situation where I like to use sole proprietorships is when hiring children in the family under age 18. I discussed this concept in Concept 6. This type of family support company can be extremely helpful for families in saving additional taxes if they can legitimately involve their children in the business. This company may also charge one of your other formal business entities to provide support and management services.

Other Considerations

DOING BUSINESS AS (DBA)

Filing a DBA is basically the method of reserving a name for your business. It truly doesn't provide any asset protection benefit and is primarily a marketing tool to reserve or protect your company name in your locale from another business using it. Remember, you don't need to complete such a filing to be "in business" in the eyes of the IRS or potential creditors; it is simply a marketing or banking necessity.

BUSINESS LICENSES

A business license may be required, depending on the type of business you operate. If you have an official location or are working out of your home, rules for a business license will vary among states, counties, and local municipalities. You will want to do some basic research to see what the requirements are for your type of business and where you operate.

EMPLOYEES

If you have employees in your business, extra licensing and insurance will be required. It still doesn't mean you have to form a formal entity; you can have employees in a Sole Proprietorship. HOWEVER, you will need to obtain a state and federal identification number, register with the requisite unemployment agency, and acquire workers' compensation insurance, just to name a few. Again, you will want to consult with your CPA and attorney, and complete some basic research about reporting requirements for having employees in your area of the country.

Partners

It may not seem like it on the surface, but a General Partnership is very similar to a Sole Proprietorship. A General Partnership is essentially taxed just like a Sole Proprietorship. They also have the same personal liability exposure, if not more. They truly hit you with a little more than you bargained for in regards to liability. You are now personally liable for the actions of your partner. Again see *Lawyers Are Liars* for an in-depth discussion of this topic. Remember, you have the same exposure to SE Tax in a General Partnership that you would have with a Sole Proprietorship.

Summary

You may start out as a Sole Proprietorship with any one of your business ventures, but please know that this time should generally be short-lived. PLEASE, if you are just getting started, I suggest you stay away from an incorporation service. There are many questions that need to be answered and instructions you should receive with the formation of your first company. I suggest you continue to meet with your CPA and attorney on at least an annual basis to make sure you are organized properly and making the transition to the correct formal entity, at the right time and in the proper place.

C-Corporation

Until 1958, the C-Corporation was the only option other than Sole Proprietorship. Maybe because of its extensive history, the C-Corporation is oftentimes oversold to small-business owners and should primarily be used by companies going public and selling stock to thousands of shareholders.

The Benefits

There are two central benefits to operating as a C-Corporation. First is the benefit of asset protection and the corporate veil. The owners and officers of a corporation are personally protected from the operations of the company, assuming they act with due care and within the scope of their duties and responsibilities.

The second benefit is ease in raising capital or, I should say, the ability to raise capital. Ease is a whole other issue. However, the C-Corporation allows you to sell stock to capitalize your business as long as you follow various securities laws and procedures in issuing stock. If you want to go down this route of selling stock to investors, you will want to get careful guidance from a securities attorney.

A third benefit that some planners suggest is that a C-Corporation is allowed to write-off more expenses than any other form of doing business. I question this argument in regards to the situation most small-business owners face and debate this in Appendix C: The C-Corp vs. S-Corp Debate—Who Wins?

The Drawbacks

The primary drawback to operating as a C-Corp is the double taxation on corporate profits. Essentially, the C-Corp pays corporate tax on its profits

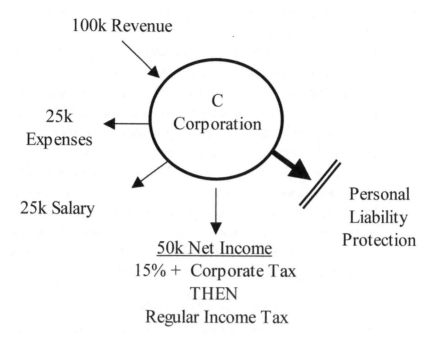

Figure B.2: C-Corporation for Operations

and then the individual shareholders pay individual income tax on the dividends they receive.

Some suggest that the cost of formation and the maintenance responsibilities are also a drawback. I suppose these may be considered a burden compared to that of a Sole Proprietorship but are generally insignificant compared to the drawback of double taxation.

In fact, I consistently argue that the requirement to have annual or regular meetings is a fantastic tax deduction opportunity and also functions to keep us thinking about our management issues (see Figure B.2).

When They Make Sense

There are really three instances when a C-Corp makes sense:

1. If you are going to go public or have more than 100 shareholders, then a C-Corp is a must. (Hint: Talk to an investment banker

before choosing this path with regard to your plans so you know what to expect about going public.)

2. If you are single and have at least $4,000 in out-of-pocket medical expenses, over and above insurance, a C-Corporation could be a good fit. It doesn't mean you still won't have an S-Corp in the mix, but it may pay to have a C-Corp for medical expenses. See the discussion on Health Reimbursement Arrangements in Appendix G: Selecting the Best Health-Care Strategy to Save Taxes.

3. Finally, maybe, just maybe, you have the right type of situation with income and expenses, and want to run your operational business as a C-Corp. It is rare that this works for my clients; I want them to make more money than the few deductions this form of business may offer them. (Hint: Run the numbers, and again see Appendix C: The C-Corp vs. S-Corp Debate—Who Wins?).

Potential Scams to Avoid

There are a number of half-truths promoters use to push their C-Corp strategy on the unwary:

1. You get better asset protection with a C-Corp than an S-Corp or LLC. Hogwash! Both give you the same asset protection. Read my book *Lawyers Are Liars* where I back up this point repeatedly with footnotes and real law.

2. You will get more write-offs with a C-Corp than an S-Corp or LLC, and thus will save taxes. Another half-truth. Yes, there are some good fringe benefit write-offs, but by the time you try to get around the corporate tax with loans, higher payroll, or a separate entity so you can run the C-Corp at zero profit, it is a complete waste of time and money. Again see Appendix C.

3. All the Fortune 500 Companies are C-Corps so you should be one, too. It's another misleading statement. Yes, all of these companies are C-Corps, but it's because they have to be. They have thousands of shareholders. You don't need these extra headaches in a small business.

4. Finally, promoters will add insult to injury and want you to form your entity in Nevada or Delaware. This is under the guise of saving state tax or because all of the Fortune 500 companies have done so. Please note that you will not save any state tax by incorporating in Nevada if you live or operate your business in a state imposing an income tax. Please see Chapter 3 in my book *Lawyers Are Liars* where I again back up my position with plenty of footnotes citing the law.

Summary

Again, if you are just getting started, I suggest you stay away from an incorporation service. There are many questions that need to be answered and instructions you should receive with the formation of your first company. Consult with the CPA that is actually going to do your tax return and show you literally how the C-Corp is going to save you taxes in years to come. Run the numbers and anticipate future profit and growth in your business and the difficulty of getting profits out of your company without paying corporate tax. With a little research and consultation, the proper entity will immediately show itself.

S-Corporation

In 1958 the S-Corporation was born. It was created specifically for small-business owners who needed asset protection but did not want to deal with the problems of double taxation and the dreaded corporate tax.

I'm convinced that the overwhelming majority of business owners creating ordinary income (commissions, sales of services, products, or 1099 income, etc.) can benefit from the S-Corporation. Moreover, these same people should stay away from the C-Corporation and only use a Limited Liability Company (LLC) for partnering with others or holding assets.

The Benefits

There are really two primary benefits to operating as an S-Corporation, although there are also a number of ancillary benefits. First is the benefit of asset protection and the corporate veil just as with the C-Corporation. Both are identical in asset protection benefits. The owners and officers of a corporation are personally protected from the operations of the company, assuming they act with due care and within the scope of their duties and responsibilities.

The second benefit, one that is unique to this form of doing business, is the ability to save on the self-employment tax. Those with an S-Corporation still need to pay their fair share of Social Security and Medicare taxes; however, they can legitimately minimize this amount by taking what is called a reasonable salary and pushing the rest of the profit out the bottom as net income.

There is no corporate tax or self-employment tax on the net income of an S-Corporation. It flows through to the individual shareholders through what is called a K-1. This form is generated when the S-Corporation files its 1120S tax return. Figure B.3 is a diagram of how this strategy plays out.

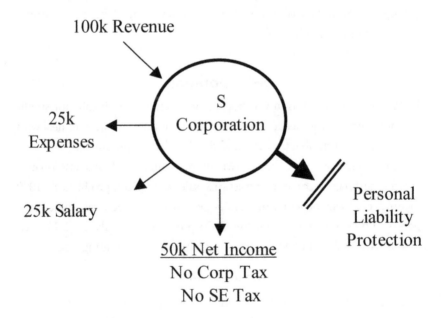

Figure B.3: S-Corporation for Operations

Reasonable Salary

This is probably one of the greatest debates in tax law when it comes to small-business owners. In fact, Congress has repeatedly tried to address this issue through legislation. On one extreme are CPAs that actually don't suggest S-Corporations at all to their clients. Maybe it's because they are too conservative, think it's too much work, or simply don't like the strategy. I don't know. But then you have the other extreme where certain planners, usually not CPAs, recommend no salary at all and abuse the system. Of course, these are the folks that are going to ruin it for the rest of us.

Bottom line, most CPAs wish that Congress and/or the IRS would simply issue some regulations with objective criteria for a reasonable salary that is justifiable and reasonable. No pun intended.

For now, it has been my consistent position (upheld under audit) that your salary level can be a percentage of your overall net income and should never be less than one-third of your total net income. In fact, at the lower levels of income your percentage of salary to net income can increase dramatically.

Therefore, as Figure B.3 shows, if your net income is projected to be $75,000, your salary should be at least $25,000. If your net income is $36,000, your salary may need to be $18,000 or higher. It simply depends on the position you and your CPA decide to take. It is truly a subjective analysis you need to complete with your tax planner.

The Drawbacks

There really aren't any significant structural drawbacks to the S-Corporation. However, if I had to pick out a few minor ones, I would mention the following three:

First, you have the formation and maintenance costs. However, these are going to be similar to the costs of a C-Corporation or LLC. These would only be a drawback if you were to compare the S-Corporation to the Sole Proprietorship.

Second, we need to discuss the payroll procedure. When you have an S-Corporation, it is absolutely critical you complete payroll reports at least quarterly. I discuss this procedure more fully below.

Finally, it's important to note that S-Corporations are really inflexible for tax planning. You almost never want to put buy-and-hold property in an S-Corporation because it is very difficult to distribute appreciated property out of an S-Corporation, and being creative with 1031 exchanges is challenging at best. It is also difficult to get creative with partners and how you distribute partnership profits. I generally suggest an LLC, or LLP for professional partners, where their individual S-Corporations are the partners and they can funnel their income through their own S-Corporation for payroll planning and various other tax strategies.

Payroll Procedures

When you have an S-Corporation, payroll becomes an important consideration. On one hand you have those payroll services and anal-retentive CPAs that want to do biweekly payroll for you and try to get you in the "take-a-paycheck" mode. This is complete overkill and a waste of your time, and generally increases the fees to those suggesting you use this format.

At the other end of the spectrum, you have advisors out there, typically not CPAs, that try to get away with doing a payroll report once a year and erroneously believe the IRS won't care that you aren't giving them their withholdings on a more regular basis. Don't make this mistake either. You are asking for an audit in this situation.

In the middle of these two extremes is where most of us reasonable CPAs operate. You simply need to do a quarterly payroll report, and you don't have to wait to take a paycheck. You take "draws" out of the S-Corporation whenever you need cash and then quarterly allocate a portion of those draws to payroll expense and send in your quarterly deposit. The IRS is satisfied with this, and you save time and money compared to either other extreme. Hint: Just get a payroll service for around $150 a quarter to take care of your payroll reporting.

When They Make Sense

It's time to get an S-Corporation when you are creating ordinary income (as defined in Concept 3 of the preceding story) and then in two instances.

The first instance when an S-Corporation makes sense is if you just need it for asset protection. You have started your business, you are creating ordinary income, and there is liability exposure. There may not be a tax reason yet, but you know that you will ultimately grow into the tax benefits and just need the protection now.

The second situation is when you will start to save on self-employment tax. I believe this is generally the case when a small-business owner has net income of at least $30,000. If the business owner has net income of less than $30,000, then the reasonable salary percentage may be too high to show significant tax savings.

Summary

The S-Corporation is for ordinary income business operations and not for holding assets. The main benefits are asset protection from the business operations and the ability to save on self-employment tax. And even if the naysayers pooh-pooh the reasonable salary procedure, the reality is that this strategy has been around a long time and many believe it will continue for many years to come. I firmly believe that even if we receive some sort of legislative guidance on reasonable salary levels, there will still be room for savings that far outweigh the cost of setup and maintenance.

Limited Liability Company

In 1977 the Wyoming State Legislature passed the first law in the United States creating the Limited Liability Company or LLC. Now they exist in every state in the country.

The main purpose of the LLC was asset protection, and that is still the case. They are not primarily built for tax planning, and there are just a few IRS rules that can make them very easy to work with. Therefore, please don't think you will get any tax benefits by forming an LLC, except for the flexibility it may afford you in a partnership situation.

The Benefits

The primary benefit of an LLC is asset protection. Thus holding assets in an LLC is what they are most commonly used for. However, it is important to note that this asset-protection benefit has numerous variations. For example, the LLC can protect "you" from a liability "in" your business, and in some states they can actually protect your assets from "your" liabilities "outside" of your LLC. Obviously, this asset protection issue is outside the scope of this particular book. I discuss this topic in Chapter 12 of my book *Lawyers Are Liars—The Truth About Protecting Your Assets.*

A secondary benefit of an LLC is the role they can play in a partnership when assigning income and expenses. From a tax perspective, an LLC is very flexible and can allocate profit or loss between partners in unique ways (something that can't be done in an S-Corporation). It's interesting to note that it is able to do this not because of some LLC tax law but because the LLC is taxed as a partnership in the eyes of the IRS.

The third significant benefit is in regards to asset protection. Partners are not liable for each other's actions if you use an LLC for the partnership. This can be a critical ancillary strategy in and of itself for using an LLC. As I mentioned earlier, the individual exposure of a general partnership can be frightening when partnering. An LLC can dramatically reduce this risk.

Figures B.4 and B.5 depict the two instances when LLCs are most commonly used.

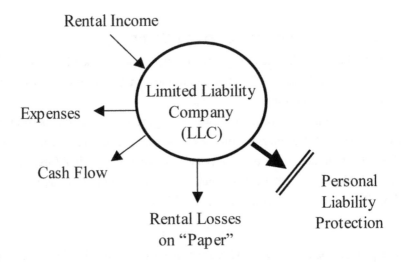

Figure B.4: LLC Holding Rental Property

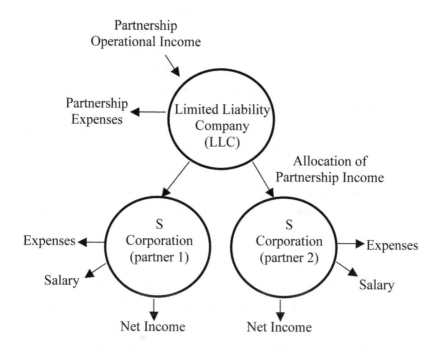

Figure B.5: LLC Operating Partnership for Ordinary Income

The Drawbacks

Really, there are not many drawbacks to the LLC except for its formation and maintenance costs. However, these are going to be similar to the costs of using a C-Corporation or an S-Corporation. These would only be a drawback if you were to compare the LLC to the Sole Proprietorship.

When They Make Sense

The two instances when an LLC makes most sense are 1) When you have an asset, for example, a rental property or investment account, and have a goal of asset protection, or 2) When you have a partnership in any sort of business venture. The LLC is essentially critical in those two situations. However, there are also a couple unique strategies that many are unaware of.

- *Single Member LLC.* This is an LLC owned 100 percent by either an individual or another entity. It can give asset protection and save you accounting fees. If you only have one owner of the company, then you don't have to do a separate tax return.
- *S-Election LLC.* Another unique characteristic of an LLC is you can "elect" them to be "taxed" as an S-Corp, if necessary. Let's say, for example, you are starting a small business and estimate that your income will be quite low in the beginning so an S-Corporation could be an unnecessary cost. You can start out as an LLC then "convert" to an S-Corporation when the time is right. This can save you a lot of money in accounting fees, but get you asset protection in the meantime.

Summary

The scary part is that an LLC can be too easy to use. Some lawyers will recommend an LLC for all their clients and then tell them to go talk to their CPAs about taxation. This type of reckless advice can cost clients a lot of wasted time and money. The LLC is so flexible it can be used in a lot of unique ways, but then it can also be used incorrectly and is difficult to unwind. Please take the time to get a tax consultation before setting up your LLC.

Limited Partnership

Limited Partnerships (LP) have been a part of this country since its formation. In fact, they were first adopted under a specific law as far back as 1673. As such, they have evolved to provide a variety of benefits in a number of situations, and although they can be very useful, they also come with some hidden drawbacks if one is not careful.

As a preliminary matter, I need to point out that an LP is made up of one or more limited partners and typically one general partner (GP). The General Partner is liable for the operations of the LP and most certainly should not be a role you serve personally. It is common practice to have a shell company or operational entity serve as GP in order to have it be the target of any potential lawsuits.

Also, you may have heard of the term FLP or Family Limited Partnership. This is essentially the same thing as an LP, except all of the Limited Partners are family members and thus may avail themselves of special IRS tax laws regarding gifting of partnership interests.

The Benefits

There are actually so many different uses for the LP, I need to list them.

- *Asset protection.* Because this is a tax book and I address this issue in *Lawyers Are Liars,* I won't go into detail regarding the asset protection benefit. Suffice it to say, it comes down to the term "charging order protection," essentially protecting the assets of the LP from outside creditors. Please note, however, that this protection varies from state to state. I include a table in *Lawyers Are Liars* showing the differences from state to state.

- *Gifting and transfer of income.* These two tax-planning benefits can be quite significant. When parents want to transfer assets to children or grandchildren, an FLP can reduce the value of an estate for estate, gift, and generation-skipping tax purposes. Past cases demonstrate that the value of FLP interest typically will be reduced by valuation discounts in the 30 to 35 percent range. Also, an FLP can shift the income tax burden from a parent who is in a high-income tax bracket to a child or other relative who is in a lower-income tax bracket.

- *Family property and parental control.* When retention of ownership of assets within the family unit is desired and a parent wants to maintain control over assets that will eventually be transferred to younger generations, the LP could arguably be the best non-tax reason for creating an FLP. The partnership agreement allows the family to keep either land or a business under the control of the family for many years to come and provides a mechanism that is much easier to control than the typical business structure or trust. This is a wonderful benefit because parents can still be in control yet at the same time get younger family members involved. Generally, the parents will be designated the general partners and other family members the limited partners.

- *Estate planning.* Finally, a parent can use an LP in order to protect assets that are being transferred to younger generations from being dissipated through mismanagement or divorce. Special provisions can be drafted into the buy-sell sections of the LP agreement requiring ownership to remain with the immediate family. Hence, if a divorce occurs in the family, it automatically triggers a buyout of certain interests so a divorced spouse will be cut out of the ownership. The LP can also be used to discourage family members from fighting over family assets and to provide a forum for the resolution of disputes among family members when they arise. Unlike an irrevocable trust created upon a parent's death, an FLP can be controlled through the vote of the family members owning the remaining partnership interests, and it increases the likelihood of keeping the assets in the family in perpetuity.

Figure B.6 depicts the general structure and shows how some of the benefits I describe above may be utilized.

The Drawbacks

In my opinion, there are really three primary drawbacks to the LP.

1. *Administrative costs.* As I discussed earlier, the basic structure of an LP requires a General Partner (GP). This GP is the liable party for the operations of the LP, which is great for the limited partners, but requires the formation of a GP entity. Now, if you already have an operational entity that doesn't have a lot of assets or equity, that's great. But if not, you have to set up a new entity that costs to form and maintain. Also, an LP must always file federal and state tax returns, where the LLC may avoid this with the single member LLC strategy (discussed above). Just keep this in mind before jumping feet first into an LP structure.

2. *Passive loss carry forwards.* As I discussed earlier, rental real estate is one of the best wealth building and tax-saving strategies in America

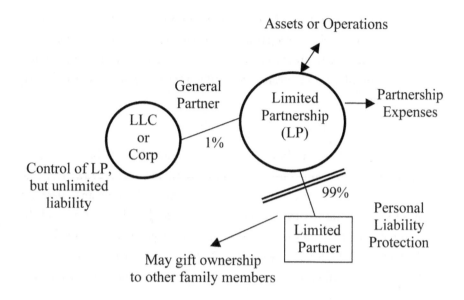

Figure B.6: Benefits of a Family Limited Partnership

today. HOWEVER, you have to be careful which entity you use to hold your rental properties. If you are generating rental losses from your properties, which is the typical situation, those losses may be deductible against other ordinary income on your tax return if you meet certain participation tests. But if your LP holds your rental properties, rather than an LLC, those losses are strictly considered "passive," and even if you qualify as a real estate professional, those losses will only be deductible against passive gains. As such, an LP is really a strong candidate to hold second homes, brokerage accounts, notes, farms, or lots, BUT not rental real estate. Be careful.

3. *Securities law.* Finally, I want to briefly mention that you need to be very, very careful regarding "partnering" with others or using "investors" in LPs. The limited partnership interest held by an investor may very likely be considered a "security" under federal and/or state security law, which will require additional duties and requirements for the promoter of the business to comply with. If

these rules during the formation and operation of the business are not followed, severe criminal and civil sanctions could be applied. Make sure to always consult with an attorney before taking money from others in a business and calling them investors or "silent partners."

Summary

Obviously, there are multiple instances where an LP could be an excellent choice for you in your business and/or assets. There also drawbacks that need to be carefully considered before embarking on the setup and operation of an LP. Generally, I feel the LP is oversold by practitioners around the country and are not properly understood by general practitioners for their true potential and drawbacks. Don't rush to set up an LP without meticulous planning regarding your objectives and its likely consequences.

APPENDIX C
The C-Corp vs. S-Corp Debate—Who Wins?

Ironically, the cost to set up and maintain an S-Corp or a C-Corp is essentially the same. Moreover, the asset protection they provide is identical. (See my book *Lawyers Are Liars—The Truth About Protecting Your Assets*.)

Nevertheless, some may be surprised to learn that from a tax perspective, which entity is better is a heated debate. In fact, many on both sides are very passionate about their opinions and fiercely defend their position. The arguments essentially boil down to this:

The advocates of the C-Corporation would argue that 1) the C-Corp offers more tax deductions to a business owner, 2) double tax can be avoided completely, 3) the lower corporate tax rates can be utilized if there is taxable income, 4) S-Corporations are on the verge of being eliminated by Congress, and 5) the salary/net-income split is oversold and a reasonable salary definition is abused.

The advocates for S-Corporations would argue that 1) the deductions for the C-Corp are limited at best for the average small-business owner, 2) the onerous double-tax problem ultimately has to be dealt with and can't be avoided, and 3) the S-Corp will continue to be utilized because the savings on FICA through a salary split is a reality.

Frankly, my opinion is the C-Corp strategy can sometimes be the better choice in certain situations. However, this is only in very limited and unique situations. In fact, I think the C-Corp strategy is oversold to the public and oftentimes by non-CPAs not realizing what they are really getting their customers into.

My partners and I have found through the preparation of thousands of individual and corporate tax returns over the years that the S-Corp is generally the best entity for the small-business owner or professional creating ordinary income.

Let me briefly address each of these arguments and suggest that you use these as a starting point for a careful consultation with your CPA or tax attorney.

The C-Corp Double Tax Can be Avoided Completely

Advocates for the C-Corp will first contend that because of all of the extra tax deductions (discussed below), there will never be a concern about double tax because the C-Corp won't have any income. I have grave concerns with this argument.

In the last argument below I clearly show that the C-Corp deductions are minimal at best and that if you have any reasonable success in your business and make money, which is the primary goal anyway, you're going to have a double-tax problem.

Seriously! Where are you going to hide all of the profit you plan on making? Invariably, when the C-Corp advocate is faced with the corporate income issue they will suggest two options: 1) take a greater salary to wipe out the income, or 2) set up multiple corporations or entities to try to hide the income.

First, let's think about the salary strategy. If you take a larger salary to wipe out the net income of the corporation, what do you pay more of? Payroll tax. You're right! That self-employment tax of 15.3 percent is what we are trying to minimize by incorporating in the first place, and if we are required to take more payroll with a C-Corp, then what's the point? In the S-Corp we could take a lower salary and not have any corporate tax on the net; obviously the S-Corp wins the argument. Pretty straightforward point.

Well, then comes the more aggressive and expensive strategy in my opinion. What some non-CPA types (typically) will recommend is setting up multiple corporations or paying fees to other companies to try to move or hide your corporate income. Can I just say the word "scary"?

The IRS has been very clear that one cannot shelter income in multiple corporations in an effort to hide income and lower tax rates. If you are ever presented with this strategy, may I say, "Run Forest, Run?" However, if you feel the argument is compelling and it makes sense, please get a second opinion from a licensed CPA that will actually sign your tax return and "run the numbers."

Finally, I would just say, "Do you really want to be maintaining more entities and sets of books in order to implement this strategy?" It can be quite an expensive proposition, and do you need this extra headache?

In my opinion, on this issue the score is S-Corp–1 and C-Corp–0.

Lower Corporate Tax Rates Can be Utilized and Are Better than Individual Rates

The next argument is that if eliminating the income doesn't work and you actually have corporate income, the C-Corp promoter will try to convince us that because the C-Corp only has a 15 percent tax rate on the first $50,000 of income and a lower rate than the personal income tax rates, you will somehow experience savings. Trust me, this is a shell game you can lose fast if you aren't very, very careful.

Now, before I get the C-Corp advocates so upset that they won't even read any further, let me say that I know there have been and may be lower tax rates on dividends from C-Corps. Also, I know that in certain situations a C-Corp can provide tremendous short-term and long-term savings. However, I think many of you must also admit that it is usually the exception and not the rule that C-Corps give the average small-business owner savings.

So, with that said, I don't think we can say that there is always a savings with the C-Corp lower tax rate, especially when income is high or tax rates change in regards to C-Corp dividend income.

This is when a classic fallback position is to "leave" money in the C-Corp because you don't want to pay the double tax. The problem with this contention is the ultimate outcome that you will have income stuck in the corporation if you pay the corporate tax and leave the net income there. Inevitably, someday you will want to get the income out of the corporation, and you will have to pay individual income tax.

Again, the advocate will come up with a Hail-Mary and argue that you can take this income as deductible personal fringe benefits out of the C-Corporation. (Again, I discuss this point more fully in the final argument.) Let me guess, these are the same folks that will sign your tax return, are going to be by your side in the audit, and will take responsibility under their malpractice insurance if they gave you bad advice? I don't think so.

Now again, IF, and I repeat IF, you are going to have minimal income and the expenses of your business will eat up all of your corporate income, then great—no problem. But heaven forbid you actually experience success in your business and make money. This double-tax threat will blindside you like a truck running a red light. Be careful, and run the numbers with a second opinion. Maybe, just maybe, do the background on your C-Corp supporter and also have them ensure in writing they will cover any penalties and interest for bad advice after they prepare your tax return and sign it!

Again, S-Corp wins the majority of the time because you don't have to worry about double-tax and profits you may be leaving in the corporation.

A C-Corp Can Have a Fiscal Year-End Different from Your Calendar Year Reporting

I won't even justify this argument with a significant discussion. If you really think that the time value of pushing income to the next tax reporting period is going to "save you money," your math is off somewhere.

Think about it. If you are delaying the recognition of income to a later tax period, then obviously you have corporate income. If you have corporate income, then you have corporate tax, which is the mess we just talked about. Then you're going to tell me that your saving interest on a tax bill that you shouldn't be paying anyway is somehow going to save you? Give me a break!

Is the S-Corp Really a Strategy That Is Here to Stay?

The C-Corp advocates have been telling me for years that the S-Corp salary/net-income split is going to get killed by Congress and/or the IRS in a matter of months.

But guess what? It hasn't been killed. It's still alive and well, and has been for 50-plus years.

Yes, in 2010 the House of Representatives kicked around a bill that would have eliminated this strategy for many small-business owners. But, the Senate voted it down, and the Senate and others, including the AICPA and numerous other lobby organizations, asked the IRS to please give us some "reasonable" salary definitions so the S-Corp strategy isn't abused.

This is what some of our politicians and the IRS are upset about: People take advantage of the S-Corp strategy and are not paying their share of FICA.

Social Security and Medicare funds are clearly not where they should be, so there are those who want to kill the S-Corp. I won't deny it. However, Congress has repeatedly asked for clearer regulations from the IRS rather than taking a large swipe at the S-Corp strategy as a whole.

My opinion is this: At the very least, use the S-Corp while it's still available. If it's modified in the future, then all of us will simply have to move over to the C-Corp. But until then, I don't want to just do nothing and sit on the sidelines paying tax in the meantime. Let's get the gettin', while the gettin' is good.

The C-Corp Offers More Tax Deductions
Than the S-Corp

This is the most technical of the arguments, so I thought I would tackle it last. For you anal accountant/engineering types, I assume you will love this.

Essentially, there is "this list" that writers in tax books will set forth that contain all of these cool tax deductions that we can only use in a C-Corp.

Now, let me say first that their point is a valid one that in an S-Corp there are certain write-offs owners can't take. Technically, the rule is that if you are a greater than 2 percent owner, you can't take these write-offs, nor can your spouse.

So here is the list:

- Disability Insurance
- Health Reimbursement Arrangement
- Day-Care Assistance Plan
- Educational Assistance Program
- Cafeteria Plan

These sounds pretty good, don't they? However, the S-Corp advocates will make four important arguments: 1) Not everyone can actually use these write-offs; 2) They don't add up to enough to make a long-term difference; 3) If you have other employees, you have to give the same benefits to them that you receive; and 4) These write-offs are even further limited if you own more than 5 percent of the corporation.

So how many of you actually are planning on paying for and can afford disability insurance? How many of you have kids in day care, or are going back to school and need a write-off for tuition other than the other write-offs available? How many of you are married and thus can completely avoid the need of a C-Corp? (See Appendix G regarding health-care strategies.)

And finally, heaven forbid you have other employees in your company, or you have a controlled group of companies with other employees for which you will be required to provide these benefits.

The list goes on and on as you get closer to the bottom line when you analyze this. I am convinced that promoters and other CPA writers on this topic fluff up and discuss the C-Corp strategy for small-business owners because they can't think of anything else to talk about, or they want to try and sell you a corporate entity setup to boot. Watch out!

But to be fair and silence the critics, I'll take a wild leap of faith and assume that you can get $15,000 more in write-offs in your C-Corp that you could get anywhere else—an assumption, I think, that is extremely aggressive. What do the numbers look like when the dust settles?

Just as before in Appendix B, let's compare apples to apples when it comes to the income and other expenses you may incur. Assume you have

$100,000 in gross income, $25,000 in general expenses, and thus $75,000 net income. Then, you take out your salary of $25,000, which you would have to do in both an S-Corp and a C-Corp. Figure C.1 is what it would look like.

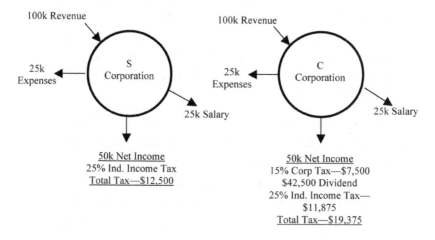

Figure C.1: S-Corp vs. C-Corp with the same amount of expenses*/**

But what if the C-Corp digs up $15,000 more in expenses? What would it look like? See Figure C.2.

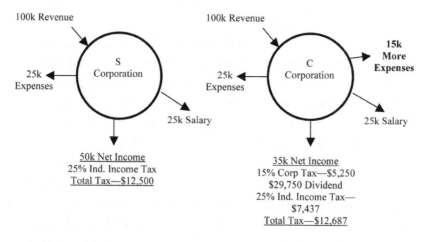

Figure C.2: Same comparison, but the C-Corp has $15,000 more in deductions*/**

* In both Figures C.1 and C.2, I assume you have an individual federal income tax rate of 25 percent. I did this to make a fair compromise. I think it is unfair to the S-Corp advocate to assume you will always be in the highest marginal individual rate and that you will get the lowest possible corporate dividend tax rate, something that fluctuates like the wind in Congress. I feel 25 percent is a good compromise.

** Moreover, you will notice I kept the corporate tax rate at 15 percent, an assumption that is fair to the C-Corp advocate. Nevertheless, heaven forbid you make more money than that in your C-Corp and have to pay a rate higher than 15 percent.

So here is the bottom line. When giving the C-Corp advocate a generous $15,000 in additional deductions and keeping tax rates fair and reasonable in the equation, it's a break-even proposition.

What this tells me is that if you have any more income in the C-Corp than expected or a lack of write-offs, you're hosed! The S-Corp wins again.

Now could you wipe out all of the corporate income? Maybe. But if not, where is the savings?

Summary

Obviously, you can probably tell that I fall into the S-Corp camp and think small-business owners should think twice, if not three times, before embarking on a C-Corp strategy. I truly discourage most small-business owners from even considering the C-Corp.

But again, are there still limited situations where a write-off for a C-Corp fits your situation perfectly? Absolutely! But they are rare, and therefore I suggest you get a second opinion before using the strategy and keep in mind it may only be a short-term strategy. Once the write-off disappears, generally you'll want to switch over to the S-Corp and use the more traditional long-term strategy of making a profit and minimizing FICA.

Bottom line, I should say too that I am not presumptuous and self-righteous enough to believe that I have presented the conclusive or absolute truth in this matter. If someone wants to echo my feelings, add some insights, or completely disagree with my analysis, I welcome your comments on my blog on this topic at WhatYourCPAWontTellYou.com.

APPENDIX D

The Business Plan

"Vital Sections to a Winning Business Plan"[1]

It is my firm belief that a Business Plan is essential to the startup of every small business. I also believe that one of the most important byproducts that can come from preparing a quality business plan is that it might prove that you shouldn't embark on a business idea. But if things look good after all the analysis, research, and building of the Plan, the results can be phenomenal!

Another critical note about a Business Plan is that they aren't just for you to use. The SBA and lending institutions require a plan before they will consider granting a small-business loan. Also, your Plan will be carefully reviewed when you are considered for any grants you may be applying for. Moreover, strategic partnerships, venture capitalists, investors, and acquiring companies will review your company's Business and Marketing Plans when considering making a deal with you.

Now surprisingly, once completed and once the decision is made to move forward, the Business Plan should actually go into the drawer. An ongoing Strategic Plan and Marketing Plan will make things happen and bring the business to life.

Your Strategic Plan (discussed later in detail) is a document you need to consistently review, modify, and revisit on a regular basis. It is essentially the "timeline" setting forth the specific tasks you need to complete in order to implement your Business Plan.

---

[1] Author's note: I use the Small Business Administration's website and printed material as a major resource in my practice for helping clients with their business plans, and also did so in writing this section of the book. I highly recommend the SBA's website sba. gov as a resource for building your business plan.

Your Marketing Plan (also discussed later in detail) is likewise an evolving document that sets forth goals, strategies, and plans you need to implement to bring in customers and those valuable sales.

I feel the critical sections of a Business Plan are as follows. You may have additional sections that your business model requires, but these are certainly the basics. Please review each one of the sections below in detail as you build your own Plan.

- Cover, Title Page, and Table of Contents
- Executive Summary
- Market Analysis
- Organization and Management
- Marketing and Sales Strategies
- Service or Product Mix
- Financials
- Appendix

Cover, Title Page, and Table of Contents

The "presentation" of the Business Plan can go a long way in showing your professionalism, the time you took to complete the plan, and your commitment to the project.

The Table of Contents is there to assist the reader in locating specific sections in your business plan. Place the Table of Contents directly following the Executive Summary and not before. Make sure that the content titles are very broad. Avoid detailed descriptions in your Table of Contents.

If you plan on giving an oral presentation of your Business Plan to bankers or investors, consider creating a PowerPoint© presentation or a DVD that can bring your product or service to life. A short video clip or pictures can say a thousand words.

Executive Summary

The Executive Summary is the most important section of your Business Plan. It provides a concise overview of the entire plan along with a history of your company. This section tells the reader where your company is and where you want to take it.

It's also the first thing your readers see, therefore it will either grab their interest and make them want to read more or make them want to put it down and forget about it. More than anything else, this section is important because it tells the reader why you think your business idea will be successful!

Some suggest the Executive Summary should be the last section you write after you've worked out all the details of your plan. The reason is that you will be in a better position to summarize your business concept after researching and writing all of the other sections. It's interesting that it's the last thing you write, but the first thing others see.

Some of the important points you should cover in the Executive Summary are:

- The Mission Statement briefly explains the thrust of your business. It could be two words, two sentences, a paragraph, or even a single image. It should be as direct and focused as possible, and it should leave the reader with a clear picture of what your business is all about. In fact, some experts suggest that the Mission Statement is just too much information for the Executive Summary and should be left inside the Business Plan.
- Names of founders and the functions they perform.
- If the business is already underway, a brief summary of the condition of the business, number of employees, sales, etc.
- Location of business and any assets, equipment, or facilities under use or needed to get started.
- Products and/or services to be rendered.
- Summary of the Marketing Plan.
- Summary of management's future plans and timeline for the business.

Don't lose sight of the fact that the Executive Summary should be a "summary" and not more than one (1) page. Most experts say *never* more than one page. With the exception of the mission statement, all of the information should be highlighted in a brief, even bulleted, fashion. Remember, these facts are laid out in-depth later in the plan.

Finally, if you can fit it in, try to give a little space to your experience and background, as well as the decisions that led you to start this particular enterprise. Include information about the problems your target market has and what solutions you provide. Show how the expertise you have will allow you to make significant inroads into the market. Tell your reader what you're going to do differently or better.

You have to convince the reader that there is a need for your service or product, then go ahead and address your future plans.

Market Analysis

The section dedicated to Market Analysis should illustrate your knowledge about the particular industry your business is in. It should also present general highlights and conclusions of any marketing research data you have collected. The specific details of your marketing research studies, however, should be moved to the Appendix of your business plan.

Experts suggest that your Market Analysis is where you illustrate your knowledge and opinions regarding your product, service, and competitors. However, you can also get in trouble here. It's important you use real data and always cite your sources. It will prevent plagiarism and also show you have really done your research with credible data.

The analysis should include an industry description and outlook, target market information, market test results, lead times, and an evaluation of your competition.

Consider the following subsections in your Market Analysis:

- *Industry description and outlook.* This overview section should include a description of your primary industry, the current size of the industry as well as its historic growth rate, trends and character-istics related to the industry as a whole (i.e., What life cycle stage is the industry in? What is its projected growth rate?), and the major customer groups within the industry (i.e., businesses, governments, consumers, etc.).

- *Identifying your target market.* Your target market is simply the market (or group of customers) that you want to focus on and sell to. When you are defining your target market, it is important to narrow it to a manageable size. Many businesses make the mistake of trying to be everything to everybody. Oftentimes, this philosophy leads to failure.

- *Market tests.* When you are including information about any of the market tests you have completed for your business plan, be sure to focus only on the results of these tests. Any specific details should be included in the Appendix. Market test results might include the potential customers who were contacted, any information or demonstrations that were given to prospective customers, how important it is to satisfy the target market's needs, and the target market's desire to purchase your business's products or services at varying prices.

- *Competitive analysis.* When you are doing a competitive analysis, you need to identify your competition by product line or service as well as by market segment. Assess their strengths and weaknesses, determine how important your target market is to your competitors, and identify any barriers that may hinder you as you are entering the market. Be sure to identify all of your key competitors for each of your products or services. For each key competitor, determine what their market share is, and then try to estimate how long it will take before new competitors will enter the marketplace.

- *Brand analysis.* A branding comparison or analysis should also be conducted for each of your competitors and their products. This will give you and your team an honest assessment of the viability of your company, products, services, and brand. It also allows you to determine the look and feel of your own brand, based on what has been successful or failed for your competitors.

- *Regulatory restrictions.* This includes information related to current customer or governmental regulatory requirements as well as any changes that may be upcoming. Specific details that you need to find out include the methods for meeting any of the requirements which will affect your business, the timing, and any costs involved.

Organization and Management

This section should include your company's organizational structure, details about the ownership of your company, profiles of your management team, and the qualifications of your board of directors.

Who does what in your business? What is their background, and why are you bringing them into the business as board members or employees? What are they responsible for? These may seem like unnecessary questions to answer in a one- or two-person organization, but the people reading your business plan want to know who's in charge, so tell them. Give a detailed description of each division or department and its function.

This section should include who's on the board (if you have an advisory board) and how you intend to keep them there. What kind of salary and benefits package do you have for your people? What incentives are you offering? How about promotions? Reassure your reader that the people you have on staff are more than just names on a letterhead.

- *Organizational structure.* Set forth the organizational structure of the business from top to bottom. A simple but effective way to lay out this structure is with an organizational chart and narrative description. This will prove that you're leaving nothing to chance. You've thought out exactly who is doing what, and there is someone in charge of every function of your company. Nothing will fall through the cracks, and nothing will be done three or four times over. To a potential investor or employee, that is very important.
- *Ownership information.* Include the legal structure of your business along with the subsequent ownership information it relates to. Have you incorporated your business? Are you using a C-Corp, S-Corp, or LLC? Or perhaps you have formed a partnership with someone. If so, is it a general or limited partnership? Or maybe you are a sole proprietor.

Important ownership information that should be incorporated into your business plan includes names of owners, percentage ownership, extent of involvement with the company, and forms of ownership (i.e., common stock, preferred stock, general partner, limited partner).

- *Management profiles.* Experts agree that one of the strongest factors for success in any startup company is the ability and track record of its owner/management, so let your reader know about the key people and their backgrounds. Provide resumés that include the following information: name, position, primary responsibilities and authority, education, unique experience and skills, prior employment, and compensation basis and levels.

- *Board of directors or advisors.* The major benefit of even an unpaid advisory board is that it can provide expertise that your company cannot otherwise afford. A list of well-known, successful business owners/managers can go a long way toward enhancing your company's credibility and perception of management expertise.

If you have a board of directors or advisors, be sure to gather the following information when developing the outline for your business plan: names, positions on the board, extent of involvement with company, background, and historical and future contribution to the company's success.

Marketing and Sales Strategies

This section is the basic framework of what will become your Marketing Plan. Your Marketing Plan will be a living, breathing document you work with monthly, if not weekly or even daily.

In this section, the first thing you want to do is define your marketing strategy. There is no single way to approach a marketing strategy; your strategy should be part of an ongoing self-evaluation process and unique to your company. However, there are steps you can follow which will help you think through the strategy you would like to use.

Use the Market Analysis that you completed for the earlier section in your Business Plan as a springboard for this section. List EVERY possible strategy that may be helpful to your business. Create a timeline of priorities based on the marketing budget and also what you hope to accomplish.

Here are some main areas of a good Marketing Plan to consider:

- Internal Procedures
- Public Relations
- Technology
- Printing and Signage
- Media

Also, each marketing strategy in your plan should include their purpose, procedure, statistical goal, and budget. (See Appendix F, The Perfect Marketing Plan, for a more detailed discussion.)

Service or Product Mix

What are you selling? In this section, describe your service or product, emphasizing the benefits to potential and current customers. Focus on the areas where you have a distinct advantage. Identify the problem in your target market for which your service or product provides a solution.

Give the reader hard evidence that people are, or will be, willing to pay for your solution. List your company's services and products, and attach any marketing/promotional materials. Provide details regarding suppliers, availability of products/services, and their costs. Also include information addressing new services or products that will be added to the company's line. Overall, this section should include:

- *A detailed description of your product or service (from your customers' perspective).* Include information about the specific benefits of your product or service. Discuss your product's/service's ability to meet consumer needs, any advantages your product has over that of the competition, and the present development stage of your product (i.e., idea, prototype, etc.).
- *Information related to your product's life cycle.* Be specific about where your product or service is in its life cycle as well as any factors that may influence its cycle in the future.

- *Any copyright, patent, and trade secret information that may be relevant.* Include information related to existing, pending, or anticipated copyright and patent filings along with any key characteristics of your products/services that you cannot obtain a copyright or patent for. Incorporate key aspects of your products/services that may be classified as trade secrets. Last but not least, be sure to add any information pertaining to existing legal agreements, such as nondisclosure or noncompete agreements.

- *Research and development activities you are involved in or are planning to be involved in.* R&D activities would include any in-process or future activities related to the development of new products/services. Include information about what you expect the results of future R&D activities to be. Be sure to analyze the R&D efforts of not only your own business but also that of others in your industry.

Financials

The financials should be developed after you've analyzed the market and set clear objectives. That's when you can allocate resources efficiently. The following is a list of the critical financial statements to include in your Business Plan.

- *Historical financial data.* If you have been in business already for some period of time, some level of historical financial data should be included (especially if they are positive). However, Business Plan consultants recommend that the most important information should be prospective in nature. Don't include too much history unless there is a specific request from an investor or creditor.

- *Prospective financial data.* All businesses, whether startup or growing, will be required to supply prospective financial data. Most of the time, creditors will want to see what you expect your company to be able to do within the next five years. Each year's documents should include forecasted income statements, balance sheets, cash-flow statements, and capital expenditure budgets. For the first year, you should supply monthly or quarterly projections. After that, you can stretch it to quarterly and/or yearly projections for years two through five.

Make sure your projections match your funding requests. Creditors will be on the lookout for inconsistencies. It's much better if you catch mistakes before they do. If you have made assumptions in your projections, be sure to summarize what you have assumed. This way, the reader will not be left guessing.

Finally, include a short analysis of your financial information. Include a ratio and trend analysis for all of your financial statements (both historical and prospective). Because pictures speak louder than words, you may want to add graphs of your trend analysis (especially if they are positive).

Appendix

The Appendix should be provided on an as-needed basis. In other words, it should not be included with the main body of your Business Plan. Your Plan is your communication tool; as such, it will be seen by a lot of people. Some of the information in the business section you will not want everyone to see, but specific individuals (such as creditors) may want access to this information in order to make lending decisions. Therefore, it is important to have the Appendix within easy reach.

The Appendix would include:

- Credit history (personal and business)
- Resumés of key managers
- Product pictures
- Letters of reference
- Details of market studies
- Relevant magazine articles or book references
- Licenses, permits, or patents
- Legal documents
- Copies of leases
- Building permits
- Contracts

- List of business consultants, including attorney and accountant

Copies of your Business Plan should be controlled. In fact, try to use a Non-Disclosure Agreement (NDA) with every Business Plan you distribute. Keep a record of everyone that receives a copy, and request its return if and when possible. Make sure recipients sign the NDA *before* they see the Plan and maybe even the Executive Summary.

Summary

I would encourage you to seek the advice of others in the preparation of your Plan and once it is finished. Find a business mentor. Choose someone you admire, who has a proven track record of success, and someone with impeccable business ethics. Ask that person to mentor you and explain that this role might require a commitment of real time and patience on their part. Follow that person's guidance and return that commitment by becoming a mentor in return. Mentors can often be found in local business groups, through your college or university, or through a friend of a friend. Be careful when choosing a mentor: Don't ask someone who, if the relationship ever sours, will cause strained family or neighborly relationships. You should also ask close friends and family to review the Plan and give you anonymous feedback if needed so you can get honest answers about your business idea and the design of your Plan. However, don't take people's opinions too personally. Remember that business is simply business.

Don't give up, and be patient. The time and season for starting a business can change. Good luck!

APPENDIX E

A Dynamic Strategic Plan

"An Essential Key to Business Success"

In my opinion, a Strategic Plan is very different from a Business Plan. A Strategic Plan sets forth a timeline of specific tasks that need to be completed in order to make your Business Plan a reality. It's a specific list of objectives to reach specific goals.

Even experienced business owners can benefit from using a Strategic Plan as an integral part of their business. It is so difficult to manage all of the loose ends and chaos that can occur when running a small business. A Strategic Plan helps tremendously.

A Strategic Plan is essentially a checklist of things that need to be completed in the next month, 3 months, 6 months, and 12 months. It takes your business plan to the next level when you are trying to decide where it is most effective to spend your time. In a lot of ways the Strategic Plan is the how-to of your Business Plan. Here are a few issues to consider before setting forth the pertinent sections of a Dynamic Strategic Plan:

- *Individual owners.* Anybody that has owned their own business knows that success can often turn on one simple principle: self-discipline. When you own your own business, there is usually no one leaning over your shoulder making sure you are working the hours you need to and focusing your energy on the right tasks. A Strategic Plan can give you a regular road map to keep you focused and help you set goals.
- *Partnerships.* A Strategic Plan in a partnership doesn't have as much to do with self-discipline as it does accountability. It is so important for partners to meet on a regular basis to discuss, strategize, decide,

assign, and then document every decision they are making as a partnership. It is so easy to forget who is doing what and why you decided on a certain course of action in the business. In difficult as well as successful times, the Strategic Plan is oftentimes the glue that can hold a partnership together.

- *Board of advisors.* Whether you are an individual owner or have partners, a Board of Advisors could be a huge resource to you in implementing your Strategic Plan, reviewing it on a regular basis, and being held accountable. This is much more than the "mentor" that may have helped you in the design of your Business Plan. This should be a group of professionals with experience and education in your industry that can give you feedback on a regular basis. At the most simplistic level, this board could be a group of family or friends you take out to dinner once a month to get their ideas and feedback, as well as report back to them regarding your accomplishments. Everyone loves to give free advice over a nice dinner. Don't underestimate the power of this resource.

- *Too much planning.* As I mentioned in the story above, a daily battle plan to spend our days most effectively can be extremely helpful. The Strategic Plan is more of a monthly procedure. There is a lot of debate as to whether or not a weekly plan is helpful or more time-consuming than it's worth. I have found that simply reviewing my monthly Strategic Plan is more than sufficient and keeps me on task each week.

Step 1. Create the Necessary Sections for Your Strategic Plan That Make Sense to You

The following sections are what I feel are the bare essentials of a good Strategic Plan and what you should consider each time you sit down to plan:

- Organizational or management issues
- Product development
- Systemization

- Personal training and education
- Employees and vendors
- Managing by statistics
- Marketing tasks (based on your Marketing Plan)

Below I have created some questions and/or topics to consider in each of the above categories. Of course these are not conclusive and just a starting point for you as you review and update your Strategic Plan on a regular basis.

- *Organizational or management issues.* Consider any legal or tax planning items that need to be dealt with. Are there facility issues to address? Are there any employees that need to be moved, trained, or terminated? What structural issues with the business need to be planned for over the next 3, 6, or 12 months?
- *Product development.* How is your product or service mix doing? Do you need to change prices, add another product or service to your lineup, or start developing something you want to roll out in the future? Could your customer service be improved upon? What needs to be modified or completely changed due to the current market and economy?
- *Systemization.* How do you deliver your products/services? Are they being delivered in the most efficient and effective manner possible? How can you improve to save time and money? EVERY employee and member of your organization needs to understand the "system" that produces your product and service, AND the role they play in that system.
- *Hatting.* This phrase has been referred to thousands of times and written about in business journals for years. Does everyone in your organization understand what "hat" they are wearing and the tasks they are to be completing each day? What are their responsibilities, and are they being held accountable to accomplish them?
- *Personal training and education.* Do you currently have all of the necessary business skills OR trade skills specific to your product mix to give a valuable final product or service? What are the next books you

plan on reading? What videos or DVDs are you watching? What is your plan for continuing education as a business owner?

- *Employees and vendors.* If you have employees, do you have a quality set of policies and procedures, and an employee handbook? Do all of your employees understand their duties and responsibilities? What are you doing in the future for training and social events? Are all of your vendors performing up to your expectations and guidelines? Do you need to send out more of your required services for "bid" to see if you can save money or get better service?

- *Managing by statistics.* Have a system to report sales, costs, production, budget-to-actual figures, etc. Have numbers for everything! Track them and manage by them. Set goals and objectives that can be tracked by objective criteria. Review these numbers every time you open your Strategic Plan. Hold yourself accountable if you're not reaching your goals.

- *Marketing tasks.* What are the items in your Marketing Plan that you need to implement now or put into your Strategic Plan for the future to make sure you follow through on them?

Step 2. Create a Timeline for All of the Action Items to Occur

Don't stress about this process. All of your objectives and tasks to complete from the different sections above should be commingled in an overall timeline. Don't set up a checklist for each category. Put them all in one master timeline that should be broken into 3-month, 6-month, and 12-month periods.

Sometimes it is important to set up weekly or monthly tasks that need to be completed when you first get started.

Step 3. Revisit your Strategic Plan Regularly

As I stated above, I suggest you update your plan monthly, and at the very least redraft it every three months. Nevertheless, you should be carrying it around with you everywhere you go. Review it constantly, and stay disciplined! Make sure you are making notes to your plan whenever you have a "brilliant idea." Don't say to yourself: "I need to do that next quarter when I review my plan." Write it down now!

Step 4. Continue to Manage by Statistics

Your numbers and reports, even if you are only keeping track and reporting to yourself, will consistently tell you if you are headed in the right direction. Don't get discouraged. Make changes as needed. Being a business owner means change. Don't be afraid of it. Embrace it, and become accustomed to it.

APPENDIX F

The *Perfect* Marketing Plan

"If you don't have this, you WILL fail"

First and foremost, I don't pretend to be a marketing genius. There are many incredible experts that have written books, teach, and consult on the topic of marketing for the small-business owner.

However, I'm convinced that millions of small-business owners don't have an affordable and practical contact to help give them support and direction in their marketing needs. Most business owners make their best guesses as to what may work for marketing and take a shotgun approach to finding a method that may work for them.

With no one to turn to, I feel the CPA can oftentimes be best suited to give their clients some initial guidance on general business management, including marketing.

Personally, I feel I have something to share in this area of business and hope that many of you find this information helpful. I have been a business owner since I was eight years old when I opened my first lemonade stand and tried to entice customers to buy my product. Today I own several businesses where I am personally involved in the marketing decisions each day, and update and maintain several Marketing Plans.

Now, what do I mean by a "Perfect" Marketing Plan? Essentially, I am trying to say that the "Perfect" plan is what is best for you in YOUR business. Every marketing plan will be different. Even businesses that are selling the same product or service may use a different strategy to reach their customers and close sales.

I simply share this section and these resources with you in the hope of helping you better reach the sales goals you have set for yourself in your own business.

Bottom line, I feel the most important step you can take to increase your sales is to develop and maintain a real plan and follow it. Here are the basic outline and steps to creating the Perfect Marketing Plan for your business:

Step 1. Establish Your Niche and Brand It

Use the research you completed in your Business Plan, or if you have been in business for some time and never went through the process of creating a Business Plan, step back and take a fresh look at your business. Be very clear with yourself about what service or product you are going to provide and why it is so special. Be prepared to brand this service or product in every possible way you can. Before you can market something, you have to be sold on it yourself as to why it is different and better than your competitors. This "difference" should be a theme in all of your marketing materials and give you a clear vision on what methods you will be using to sell it and why.

Step 2. Define Your Target Customers

Using the product mix created in your Strategic Plan, define your target customers. Who is going to purchase your services or products? Describe them in detail. Where and how are you going to find them? What are their purchasing habits, and how are you going to fill that niche or need? What is the best price for your services or products based on your target customer?

Step 3. Build Your Plan

Using some of the following sections and ideas, build a list of marketing strategies that you are already using and that you may want to implement in the future. Don't leave anything off the list. Even if you don't have the budget or time for it right now, write it down so you can work toward employing some of them in the future.

Internal Procedures

- *Customer database management.* Maintain a master database of all prior, current, and potential customers with all of their contact information, especially their e-mail addresses. You will use this for consistent follow-up and other marketing strategies.

- *Customer thank-you program.* Implement a regular procedure for sending thank-you cards, e-mails, and texts, or making phone calls to thank customers for purchasing services or products, as well as for referrals. Consider a service such as sendoutcards.com.

- *Customer holiday and birthday contact list.* Choose which customers you want to send gifts, cards, e-mails, or even texts to on specific holidays or for their birthdays or special events.

- *ABC client rating system.* Prioritize your clients or customers if possible and establish certain procedures and protocol for each group. Obviously, give your "A" clients more attention than your "C" clients and allocate your resources and marketing budget wisely.

- *Customer referral program.* Create a reward or incentive program for customers that refer others to your company. Give such rewards only after their referrals actually complete the purchase cycle, although you still may send them a thank you.

- *Staff referral program.* If you have employees, create a reward or bonus program to incentivize your internal staff to find customers and refer them to your business. Maybe even consider internal contests and prizes as part of the plan.

- *Strategic partnerships.* Immediately begin to maintain a list of all possible referral partners that may be vendors or businesses working in your same industry that view you as a strategic alliance and not a competitor. Consistently reach out to them with referrals of your own and generous thank yous for referrals in return.

- *Re-activation mailings, phone calls, and scheduling.* Many small *and* large businesses forget that their prior customers can be where some of their greatest future sales may be. Have a system to follow up and contact them with new services and products.

- *Customer surveying and success story utilization.* Potential customers are intrigued with the testimonials of a company's satisfied customers. This tool can oftentimes cause a customer on the fence to buy.

Public Relations

- *Branding all company materials and marketing activities.* Companies have to have a brand. One of the age-old techniques in advertising is TOMA—Top of Mind Awareness. You want potential customers to think of you first when they think of your type of service or product. Branding is a key part of this technique.
- *Contests and events.* Consider having contests for customers that create interest in and loyalty to your company. Sporting events provide a great source for this type of marketing. Golf tournaments, March Madness pools (without betting), tickets to concerts or events, and raffles are some options.
- *Seminars or workshops.* Having regular live events where customers can get additional information or you can reach potential customers can be extremely powerful in a marketing plan. Make sure you look at all of the costs of holding such events and the marketing needs to get them into the seats. It can be a budget buster if you aren't careful.
- *Charitable activities.* More and more customers today want to see a company's commitment to "giving back." Choose a charity that you want your employees and customers to support through purchasing your services and products. This could even be an effort to protect the environment and creating some type of "green" aspect to your business.

Technology

- *Monthly e-newsletter.* A regular publication, whether e-mailed or printed and mailed, is an excellent strategy to stay in contact with your customers. Look into a program like Streamsend.com to efficiently send out your e-mails. Just don't overdo it with spam, and make sure your newsletter has useful and interesting content *every* time.

- *Monthly e-seminar.* Some businesses can benefit from an e-seminar or webinar strategy. If you are a service-based business with a variety of services and changing laws or there are constant changes in the industry, a webinar can help your key people brand themselves with the customers and create more customer loyalty.
- *Website maintenance and design.* EVERY business needs a website today, even if it is simply a destination page with a basic description of the products and services offered and contact information. Make sure it looks up-to-date and professional at all times.
- *SEO (Search Engine Optimization).* If the web is where you look for a lot of your customers, then SEO programming is absolutely critical. Have the right people to succeed at this strategy.
- *Pay-per-click campaigns.* The PPC strategy is similar to SEO, but very different in impact. It can be expensive, but if it is built into the cost of sales and is targeted, it can catapult your business to incredible levels of success.
- *Social networking (Facebook, LinkedIn, and Twitter).* It's clear that social networking doesn't help every business, but it can be a tremendous help to certain types. Make sure you aren't just having fun and are actually promoting your business without driving your contacts crazy. It can be a huge time sucker.
- *YouTube videos, podcasts, and apps.* Video and audio recordings may be a way for you to attract more customers to your business from the web. Also, your business may be able to create an application for a smart phone that can generate revenue, or at the least put your name in front of millions, if it is done right. Consider testing some of these strategies if your research shows your customers may find you from one of these mediums.

Printing and Signage

- *Brochures, fliers, and business cards.* While some businesses are web based and don't need print material, others have customers walking into their business every day. Having something for them to walk away with is absolutely critical. Take the time to have such materials always look professional and reflect your branding and the theme of your Marketing Plan.

- *Signage.* Don't underestimate the power of good signage. This could include a billboard, the sign on your building, wrapping your car with your logo or business name, road signs, etc. There are a number of options. Meet with a local sign/printing company for ideas and costs.

Media

- *Radio and TV.* Some businesses can afford radio and TV advertising. In smaller local areas, it can actually be quite affordable. Look into it, and at least get a quote if you think it could reach your target market.
- *Newspaper, magazines, and coupon packs.* Depending on your target market, spending some time and money in this area could be a huge benefit or useless cost. Do some test marketing before committing to long-term contracts.
- *Yellow Pages.* In some areas the printed Yellow Pages are still used and a good investment in your marketing budget. However, new online Yellow Page strategies can be much more affordable and helpful to your business. More and more people are going to the web just to find what local products and services are available.

Step 4. Detail the When, Where, and How of Each Strategy

Under each marketing strategy in your Plan, include four important details regarding how each strategy will be implemented:

1. *Purpose.* What is the purpose of this marketing strategy? Who will it target and why?
2. *Procedures.* What specifically needs to be completed? Who is going to do it and when? Is it going to be you, an employee, or outsourced?

3. *Statistical goals.* Remember, you are managing by statistics! There needs to be objective numerical data to confirm the success or failure of this strategy. Find it, and use it weekly or AT LEAST monthly.

4. *Budget.* How much is this strategy going to cost? Is it one time, weekly, monthly, or annual? Nail it down, and review it regularly.

Step 5. Track Where Your Customers Are Coming From

If you are aren't tracking where your new customers came from, your marketing budget could well be money spent in vain. Be religious about asking every one of your new customers where they heard about your company and what made them come to you. Ask them their opinion about your marketing pieces, if possible.

FINALLY, remember that the list above and the procedures for implementing these strategies are by no means conclusive. ANYTHING is fair game for your Marketing Plan. I urge you to be as creative as possible! The important thing is to set SPECIFIC tasks and deadlines to implement your plan, and TRACK the success of each strategy.

APPENDIX G

Selecting the Best Health-Care
Strategy to Save Taxes

A s I discuss in Concept 7 of the story, there are several strategies to consider when it comes to tax planning and our health care. Regrettably, millions of Americans aren't aware of these tactics and CPAs aren't talking about them as much as they should be with their clients.

When it comes to writing off our health care there are really only four options. I guess five, if you count not even trying, but here is a brief description of the four that actually may work for you in your situation.

1. *Itemizing.* This is the method of reporting your total medical expenses as an Itemized Deduction on your Schedule A of your 1040. The problem with this technique is that the deduction is limited and you can only deduct those expenses over 7.5 percent of your Adjusted Gross Income (AGI). So, effectively this means if you make $100,000 as your AGI, and you have $8,000 in medical expenses, you can only deduct $500 (the amount over 7.5 percent of your AGI or $7,500). It's ridiculous! Itemizing is really the worst possible option and it rarely works for the average taxpayer. In fact, some studies report that over 95 percent of Americans "try" to itemize and have no success whatsoever. I try to use any of the remaining three strategies for my clients and only use itemizing as a last resort.

2. *Flexible Spending Account or FSA.* Many people know this as the "use it or lose it" cafeteria option. This essentially involves an employee choosing a certain amount to be withheld from their paycheck (before taxes), and having those funds set aside in their

FSA. Then, the employee needs to pull those monies out of the FSA for qualifying medical expenses before year-end. If they don't pull out all of the money, then the monies are lost and forfeited back to their employer. I don't think this is a terrible strategy, so long as my clients don't leave any money in the FSA at year-end. I tell my clients if they can participate in an FSA, go for it—just use the funds. Admittedly, it is a little nerve-racking for my clients to use this strategy, but it can still be worth it.

3. *Health Reimbursement Arrangement or HRA.* This strategy can only be used by small-business owners, and if I can get my client into an HSA strategy (discussed below), I won't even suggest the HRA. Nevertheless, they can still be useful and are used when I have clients with high medical expenses. Some families have very high medical expenses due to prescription drugs, permanent medical conditions, disabilities, or handicapped children. This is a fantastic method to get some deductions, but again they have to have a small business to make it work. As I mentioned in Appendix C debating the benefits of a C-Corp, this is the one area where a C-Corp may actually make sense. However, if my client is married, I can accomplish the HRA strategy without using a C-Corp. Here are two diagrams illustrating the two methods when either married or single:

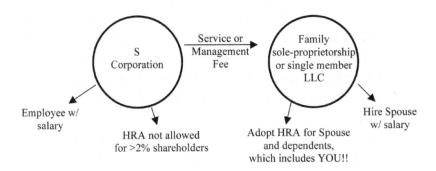

Figure G.1: HRA Strategy if Married

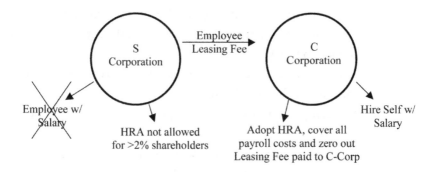

Figure G.2: HRA Strategy if Single

In summary, remember you must have a profitable small business to implement the HRA, you should have medical expenses of at least $4,000 (or more) a year to justify the additional administrative cost of the structure, and get some professional advice regarding your situation. Run the numbers and make sure your advisor understands the documentation and reporting requirements. The HRA isn't particularly expensive or difficult to implement, but this is something the average person shouldn't try to figure out on their own. Get some technical support and guidance if you think the HRA is a potential strategy for you.

4. *Health Savings Account or HSA.* My favorite strategy for my clients, when possible, is utilizing the HSA. These plans are tax-favored savings accounts combined with a qualifying high-deductible health insurance plan. They allow taxpayers to deposit tax-deductible funds into a health savings account that can be used to cover medical costs (the contribution limits change each year and are adjusted for inflation, but are generally similar to IRA contribution amounts). You don't have to have a small business to set up an HSA, however, you must have a qualifying high-deductible insurance policy. There are several key benefits of an HSA I think are amazing:

  • You save money on your insurance premiums with the high-deductible insurance.

- The HSA contribution is deductible on the front page of your tax return and is not affected by AMT adjustments or how much money you make.
- If you don't use the money in the HSA by year-end, it carries forward for the rest of your life
- You can pull out the money for qualifying health-care expenses tax free
- If you don't want to use the funds for health care, you can pull out the funds like a traditional IRA and pay taxes after you turn 59 ½.
- You can invest the money in essentially anything and grow the account tax-free.
- Finally, the HSA enables you to take control of your own health-care decisions because you are paying directly for your medical care out of your savings account.

Now, although the HSA sounds like a no-brainer, like any insurance plan or tax strategy, one needs to do their research and understand all of the ramifications of implementing such a plan. The insurance plan options and issues can be the most daunting to understand, and most people are immediately concerned about a higher deductible and what that could mean if a big medical bill arose. However, once they understand that the savings in premiums could easily exceed the higher deductible and those funds can be set aside in a tax-deductible and tax-free growth scenario, the concerns seem to fade away. Bottom line, do your research and talk with a tax planner and insurance planner that advocate the HSA so you don't get steered into a plan where you just end up trying to itemize your medical expenses, and end up nowhere.

See Figure G.3 to help you better understand the difference between these three main types of plans.

	Flexible Spending Arrangement (FSA)	Reimbursement Arrangement (HRA)	Health Savings Account (HSA)
Overview	An employer-funded arrangement under a cafeteria plan that is a "use it or lose it" salary deferral by the employee	An employer-funded benefit plan without any salary reduction that reimburses employees for qualified medical expenses	A savings account created in conjunction with a high-deductible health ins. plan ("HDHP") to pay for medical expenses
Eligibility	C-Corporation employees, non-owner employees of an LLC or sole prop., less than 2% shareholders of an S-Corporation	C-Corporation employees, non-owner employees of an LLC or sole prop., less than 2% shareholders of an S-Corporation	Any individual covered under a HDHP, under age 65, and not covered under a non-qualifying health insurance plan
Funding	Employee-funded out of salary; employer sets limit	Employer-funded and employer sets amount	Employer- and/or employee-funded
Health Plan Requirements	None	None	Must be HDHP; amounts adjust each year
Contribution Limits	Unlimited; employer determines amount	Unlimited; employer determines amount	Amounts adjust each year

Figure G.3: Three Main Types of Plans

	Flexible Spending Arrangement (FSA)	Reimbursement Arrangement (HRA)	Health Savings Account (HSA)
Tax Treatment	Employer may deduct any contributions; non-taxable to the employee; no payroll tax withholding	Employer may deduct any contributions; non-taxable to the employee; no payroll tax withholding	Employer may deduct any contributions; not subject to payroll tax withholding; employee contribution is deductible on the front page of the 1040
Carryover and Investment	Lose unused funds; no investment options	No carry forward of reimbursement amount; no investment options	Unused funds carry forward; funds may be invested and self-directed
Administration	Employer-administered	Employer-administered	Third-party administered

Figure G.3: Three Main Types of Plans, continued

APPENDIX H
The Strategic CPA

Choosing the right CPA is clearly a challenging situation. You want to find one that communicates well, brings strategies to your attention on a regular basis, is affordable, and is also willing to adjust to your risk tolerance (within reason).

I know that many of you either out of self-confidence OR apathy with the accounting profession have even chosen to prepare you own tax return with some of the popular software out there. OK, I'll say it: Turbo Tax©.

However, I would like to strongly encourage you to at least have a CPA "review" your tax return if you want to prepare it yourself, and at the very least have a semi-annual planning session to make sure you aren't missing anything.

I know I am preaching to the choir to many of you that certainly know having a good CPA is priceless. You just need to find the right one.

Therefore, I have compiled what I feel are some key characteristics of a strategic CPA. And let me explain why I use the word "strategic" in my description of a quality CPA.

I think a quality CPA's most important skill is to be strategic on your behalf. It doesn't just mean bringing you good ideas. They should have good entrepreneurial skills, be able to communicate well, and have an efficient team behind them to complete the work.

When you bring all of these characteristics together, you have someone that is "strategizing" on your behalf and creating the maximum possible savings for you in your quest to live the American Dream.

Interview as many CPAs as you need to, and analyze them against the characteristics discussed below.

- *They're not perfect.* If they think they are perfect, you've got the wrong CPA. Remember, not one person can encompass all of these characteristics. Ask them what their weaknesses are. If they're good they will admit that with their team they are better than their own personal skills or style. Be patient. They should be busy, and they won't be cheap. However, they should be affordable.

- *They can answer the questions that you have learned in this book.* If you start asking them questions about the topics of this book and they have the deer-in-headlights look or say they have to go research basic questions, you've got the wrong CPA. My book is not that complex. I'll argue with any CPA, anytime, that they should at the least be discussing the strategies in this book with their clients, if not recommending them.

- *They are willing to share your risk tolerance.* If they won't be flexible, you've got the wrong CPA. You will never find a CPA that shares your risk tolerance exactly. They should be willing to be creative yet not be too risky; at the same time they shouldn't be too conservative. You will want to ask them how they would treat certain kinds of deductions, income, or strategies to see if they respond to your satisfaction.

- *You can understand them.* If you can't understand a word they're saying, you've got the wrong CPA. I'm not just talking about language barriers either. If you're confused after a conversation with your CPA, keep interviewing until you can find one that is at least remotely interesting or enjoyable to talk with.

- *They have an entrepreneurial spirit.* If they think that having a small business is a bad idea, you've got the wrong CPA. In fact, unless you are 82 years old, they should at least be discussing the options of owning a small business and how it could help you save taxes. Some CPAs don't like small businesses, and they would rather just deal with people who have W-2 income. This isn't the CPA for you if you really want to save and build wealth.

- *They invest in real estate.* If they aren't suggesting you buy rental property, at least to some degree, you've got the wrong CPA. Now, I realize that there is a time and a season for everyone in regards to real estate. Sometimes it isn't the right time to buy; it's the right time to sell or just sit back and collect rent. However, I'm convinced that anyone interested in really building wealth and/or retirement income must consider real estate in the equation.

- *Their team is better than they are.* As I stated above, if your CPA thinks he's better than his team or plans on doing all of the work him or herself, you've got the wrong CPA. Remember that you will be working with a CPA that gives you strategies and leads a team. They shouldn't be preparing your tax return and inputting your data. That is a poor use of their time. They should be strategizing with you and reviewing your tax return. With that in mind, analyze the office staff and how they answer the phone and interact with you. These are the people you will be talking with more than your CPA. If they aren't cordial, kind, and helpful, it indicates there are problems.

APPENDIX I
Maximizing Write-Offs: A List You Have to Have!

Everywhere I go, every time I speak at an event, and even at dinner with friends, I constantly get asked the question: "So what's a write-off?"

Well, surprisingly, there isn't some master list included in the Internal Revenue Code, or even created by the IRS. There is simply the tax principle set forth in Code Section 62 that a valid write-off is any expense incurred in the production of income.

So some may say, "Well Mark, prepare a list of what you think is deductible and I'll rely on that." I have included such a list (see below), but it is really more than that.

There are some critical approaches to your behavior that can help you maximize your deductions and save you thousands of dollars a year and much, much more over a lifetime.

As I discussed in the preceding story, a good CPA should be teaching their clients to think above the line. That line is your Adjusted Gross Income or AGI. That is the number in the bottom right-hand corner on the front page of your tax return. What I mean by thinking above this line is constantly trying to think of any and all personal expenses that may have a business purpose. So many Americans blindly pay taxes, then pay for every one of their personal expenses "after taxes." With a small business venture in your life and on your tax return, you can regularly succeed at converting personal expenses to business expenses.

Seasoned business owners over the years get proficient at keeping good records and thinking of a business purpose for many of their expenses. They have changed their behavior. They have become entrepreneurs and use that mentality in all of their purchases. Frankly, I have fallen in love with this approach to purchases and saving money.

Over the years my attitude about this has driven my wife crazy. She has consistently asked, "Do we have to find a tax reason for every one of our purchases?" I don't think this is a particularly annoying habit, but that's just me. I suggest you get in the practice. A penny saved is a penny earned.

So with all of that said, here is the list. Remember, it's just a start, and not every one of these items is always a deduction. It can depend on the character of your business and the overall approach to designing your tax return. Nevertheless, try to track every expense you can and comb over them with your CPA at the end of the year.

All necessary business expenses	Internet hosting and services
Accounting fees	Investment advice and fees
Advertising	Laundry while traveling
Amortization	License fees
Annual meetings	Lobbying (if qualifying)
Attorney's fees	Magazines
Auto expenses	Management fees
Bad debts (if previously income)	Materials
Banking fees	Maintenance
Board meetings	Medical expenses (with plan)
Building repairs and maintenance	Membership dues
Cafeteria plan (requires plan)	Moving
Casualty damages	Newspapers
Charitable deductions	Office supplies and expenses
Child care (requires plan)	Outside services
Cleaning/janitorial	Payroll taxes for employees
Collection expenses	Parking
Commissions to outside parties	Pension plans
Computers and tech supplies	Periodicals
Consulting fees	Postage

Continuing education	Publicity
Conventions and trade shows	Prizes for contests
Cost of goods sold (if have inventory)	Real estate related expenses
Depletion	Rebates on sales
Depreciation	Rent
Dining	Repairs
Discounts to customers	Research and development
Dues (professional or club)	Retirement plans
Education asst. (requires plan)	Royalties
Embezzlement losses	Safe-deposit box
Employees	Safe
Entertainment	Storage rental
Equipment	Subcontractors
Exhibits for publicity	Taxes
Family members on payroll	Theft
Freight or shipping costs	Telephone
Furniture and fixtures	Tolls
Gifts (within limits)	Travel
Group insurance (if qualifying)	Unemployment compensation
Health insurance	Utilities
Home office	Website design
Interest	Workers' compensation

ONLINE VIDEOS TO SAVE YOU MORE IN TAXES, BUILD YOUR WEALTH, AND PROTECT YOUR ASSETS!

- The first critical concepts in saving taxes
- Tax strategies that don't involve a small business
- Choosing the correct entity at the right time for your business
- Killer small business tax deductions and bookkeeping basics
- Designing a Business Plan for investors and the bank
- Strategic planning for business success
- Building and implementing a Marketing Plan
- The power of rental real estate—tax benefits and building wealth
- Hiring family members in your business
- Health-care strategies for a lifetime of savings
- Self-directing your retirement plan—the possibilities
- Real asset protection and how it works
- Estate Planning and why it matters

For Online Videos and Live Events visit:

MarkJKohler.com

WHAT PEOPLE ARE SAYING . . .

"I can say without reservation, after 30 years as a business owner/contractor, that I was amazed at the amount of new information he presented that actually excited me about our tax and legal futures. I also found him to be one of the most gifted and entertaining teachers I've ever been fortunate to learn from. Anyone considering attending one of his events should just go! The price to attend can't match the costs of missing Mark's incredible insights."
—RON ROPER, LUXURY OUTDOOR LIVING

"Mark is one of the smartest, funniest, and most knowledgeable people I've ever had the honor of meeting. His book *Lawyers Are Liars* is a must read and his financial and legal advice is priceless!"
—JACLYN MORATH AURORA, IL

"I've never encountered anyone who could take a dry subject like taxes and make it not only interesting but fun. When I finished Mark's class I started looking for the things he spoke about so I could use them in my tax strategy. Amazing teacher!"
—DAWNE MCELMEEL FASANELLA, BARTLETT, IL

"I saw Mark in Seattle Washington in 2008, and he was so fun and animated and full of enthusiasm. I really enjoyed him a lot!"
—JAMES TYREE, PORTLAND, OR

"Thank you Mark, I am a very happy client. Looking forward to taking one of your classes again. 'Tax and Legal' rocks!"
—SHIRI PRASAD, SACRAMENTO, CA

"I have listened to several of Mark's presentations on legal and tax strategies. They are eye-openers and provide practical business sense for businesses preferring to make intelligent, informed decisions. They are priceless!"
—DR. VANESSA VOLLMER, MISSION VIEJO, CA

"If you haven't had the opportunity to take any of Mark's classes, you are missing out. Mark' book is just on! You must have Mark and his team as your team. You will feel that all of your worries are lifted from your shoulders!"
—NANCY FONG, YORBA LINDA, CA

"We learned more from Mark in one class than all of the books we had read previously. Looking forward to our next class with him."
—BRYON HARRISON, POLSON, MT

"Any chance you get to listen to Mark will absolutely save you money and make you more intelligent!"
—DAVID K BOSTICK, HOUSTON, TX

Get Entrepreneur Magazine to help grow your business

Don't miss out on must-have tips, techniques, trends and strategies that business owners need to help build and grow their businesses. Learn what other smart business owners know. Subscribe to *Entrepreneur*!

More from Entrepreneur

Entrepreneur. Press

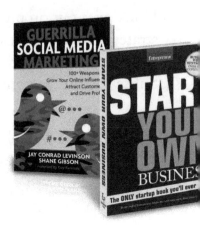

Entrepreneur Press is a leading SMB publisher, providing aspiring, emerging and growing entrepreneurs with actionable solutions to every business challenge—ultimately leading you from business idea to business success.

▣ More titles from Entrepreneur Press
http://www.entrepreneurpress.com/

Entrepreneur.com

Entrepreneur.com is the most widely used website by entrepreneurs and leaders in business worldwide. As the leading small business website, Entrepreneur.com serves its visitors' needs by creating the most satisfying experience with relevant content, logical information management and ease of access.

▣ Visit Entrepreneur.com
http://www.entrepreneur.com/

http://newsletters.entrepreneur.com/

Sign Up for the Latest in:

▣ Online Business   ▣ Sales & Marketing
▣ Franchise News   ▣ Growing a Business
▣ Starting a Business   ▣ Hot Off EPress